SPECIAL FORCE:
SOE and the Italian Resistance 1943–1945

MALCOLM TUDOR

WITHDRAWN

EMILIA PUBLISHING

Copyright © Malcolm Tudor 2004

All Rights Reserved

No part of this book may be reproduced in any form,
by photocopying or by any electronic or mechanical means,
including information storage or retrieval systems, without
permission in writing from the copyright owner and publisher
of this book

ISBN 0-9538964-2-0

Swindon Borough Council Library Services	
Askews	
	£9.99

First published in 2004 by
EMILIA PUBLISHING
Woodlands, Bryn Gardens, Newtown
Powys, SY16 2DR

Contents

Acknowledgements v

Preface vii

1   The Art of Guerrilla Warfare 1

2   Beyond the Wire 7

3   Maryland 16

4   The Italian Resistance 23

5   Secret Air Missions 34

6   The SAAF Liberators 43

7   The Ossola Rising 51

8   Cherokees in Piedmont 61

9   From the Mountains to the Sea 70

10 The Grand Finale 81

Bibliography 89

Index of names 91

Other books by Malcolm Tudor:

British Prisoners of War in Italy: Paths to Freedom

Escape from Italy, 1943–45: Allied Escapers and Helpers in Fascist Italy

Also published by Emilia Publishing

Acknowledgements

I would like to thank veterans of the campaign in Italy and their relatives who have provided me with information, especially: Oscar D'Alcorn and Victor Walker for their accounts and Miles Goldingham for that of his father, Michael, which appear in Chapter 2, William Pickering, MM, for the comments quoted in Chapter 5, and Mrs Anne Storm for the facts leading to the inclusion in the book of Chapter 6.

Preface

Special Force – or No. 1 Special Force in full – was the cover name of the Italian offshoot of Britain's secret sabotage and subversion agency: the Special Operations Executive or SOE.

The parent body was created in a hurry in the summer of 1940, just after the Dunkirk evacuation and the fall of France. Less than six weeks earlier Italy had entered the war on the German side. SOE operated in Italy and her colonies for the next three years, but it was the dramatic military and political events in the country during the second half of 1943 which led to the formation of Special Force in liberated territory in the south.

For the rest of the war, SOE's Italian branch was a key element in the campaign of guerrilla warfare waged by the Resistance against the Germans and fascists. As we shall see, the struggle also involved secret agents from the American Office of Strategic Services, the OSS, and the extensive use of Allied airpower.

In telling the story of Special Force and the Italian Resistance, I have used Italian as well as British, Commonwealth and American sources, concentrating on the individual stories which inform and enrich the wider historical narrative.

Malcolm Tudor

Newtown, Powys
September 2004

1
The Art of Guerrilla Warfare

'And now set Europe ablaze.' Winston Churchill's stirring words to Hugh Dalton, his Minister of Economic Warfare, launched Britain's agency for irregular warfare. It was 16 July 1940 and the Labour politician had just been designated chairman or political head of the new executive, one of nine wartime secret services.

Three days later, Churchill's predecessor as Prime Minister, Neville Chamberlain, now Lord President of the Council, told the War Cabinet:

> 'An organisation is being established to coordinate all action, by way of subversion and sabotage, against the enemy overseas. This organisation will be known as the Special Operations Executive.'

The project was approved on 22 July and implemented in record time.

The British Government had begun to plan for covert operations as early as 1938. SOE was born out of the fusion of three Whitehall bodies: the sabotage division of the Secret Intelligence Service, D Section, a propaganda department at the Foreign Office, Electra House, and a branch of the War Office known as MI(R) or Military Intelligence (Research), which studied guerrilla methods.

In charge at MI(R) was Lieutenant Colonel JFC Holland, DFC. He had recruited two able assistants: Brevet Lieutenant Colonel Colin Gubbins, MC, and Major Millis Jefferis. In May 1939, they published three pamphlets of practical advice and technical information for the Resistance fighter: *The Art of Guerrilla Warfare* and *The Partisan Leader's Handbook* by Gubbins, and *How to Use High Explosives* by Jefferis.

The nine points of the Guerrilla's Creed, set out in *The Art of Guerrilla Warfare*, are:

(a) Surprise first and foremost, by finding out the enemy's plans and concealing your own intentions and movements.
(b) Never undertake an operation unless certain of success owing to careful planning and good information. Break off the action when it becomes too risky to continue.
(c) Ensure that a secure line of retreat is always available.
(d) Choose areas and localities for action where your mobility will be superior to that of the enemy, owing to better knowledge of the country, lighter equipment, etc.
(e) Confine all movements as much as possible to the hours of darkness.
(f) Never engage in a pitched battle unless in overwhelming strength and thus sure of success.
(g) Avoid being pinned down in a battle by the enemy's superior forces or armament: break off the action before such a situation can develop.
(h) Retain the initiative at all costs by redoubling activities when the enemy commences counter-measures.
(i) When the time for action comes, act with the greatest boldness and audacity. The partisan's motto is 'Valiant yet vigilant.'

SOE's basic training owed much to the pamphlets. They were also translated into at least 16 languages, including Italian, and were intended to be the field service regulations for guerrilla warfare. In November 1940, Colin Gubbins was promoted to brigadier and joined SOE as Director of Operations and Training. When an acting Major General in 1943, he was appointed Executive Director or CD, a post he held for the rest of the war.

SOE moved to 64, Baker Street, London, in October 1940, close to the fictitious lodgings of Conan Doyle's Sherlock Holmes at 221B. The SOE staff soon became known as the 'Baker Street Irregulars' after the street urchins recruited by Holmes. In *A Study in Scarlet* he tells Watson:

> 'The mere sight of an official-looking person seals men's lips. These youngsters, however, go everywhere and hear everything. They are as sharp as needles too, all they want is organisation.'

Hugh Dalton also valued personnel. In August 1940, he said that 'the selection of the right men is even more important than the creation of the right machine.' SOE had been given the power to demand officers and men from all three armed forces and elsewhere. About 70 per cent came from the British Army. The rest were recruited through the old-boy network. Senior staff were invariably drawn from public schools and older universities. Those not regular officers were usually from the City and the legal, teaching and journalistic professions. In contrast, the agents came from a wide variety of social and political backgrounds and were of diverse nationalities. The only common factor was their eagerness to take action against the Germans and their collaborators.

SOE reached its maximum strength in October 1944, when the British component was just under 13,000, including about 3,200 women. Four thousand and forty two of the total were involved in the Mediterranean theatre.

According to Professor Michael Foot, historian of SOE, 5,000, mostly men, were agents on operations or waiting to go, with the rest engaged in administration, intelligence, operations, planning, research, security, signals, supply and transport.

An Italian department known as J Section was set up at the London Headquarters in October 1941 under Lieutenant Colonel CL Roseberry. His main priority was political subversion in cooperation with the Italian clandestine opposition. This was made easier by the creation of the Action Party in 1942, a militant coalition formed by the *Giustizia e Libertà* (Justice and Liberty) organisation and other like-minded groups. The party was inspired by the vision of a republican and secular state, with a large measure of local autonomy and agricultural and industrial reform.

Implementing SOE policy for Italy was mainly the duty of John McCaffery, the affable Irishman who headed the mission at the British Legation in the Swiss capital, Berne. Supplies intended for dissident groups were smuggled across the Alps or dropped by RAF aircraft, but it was eventually discovered that Italian Military Intelligence and the fascist police had penetrated the operation. The British lost some valuable supplies and were taken in by a great deal of false intelligence, but fortunately the genuine opposition was largely unscathed.

The undermining of Italian morale by radio broadcasts, leaflets, and the spreading of false rumours met with some success as Italian forces faced defeats abroad and conditions for civilians deteriorated at home. The results of other activities were harder to assess. An SOE report said:

'A certain amount of sabotage and labour strife was reported, but the chief value of this spade work was the maintenance of the spirit of anti-fascism and the creation of contacts which proved exceedingly useful later.' [1]

Through go-betweens, SOE had kept in touch with members of the Royal Family, the Vatican, army circles and even neo-fascists, as well as left-wing politicians. Proposals for a *coup d'état* in Italy supported by Allied landings were forwarded to the British War Cabinet as early as January 1943, but were rejected in line with the demand made public a few days later at Casablanca by Churchill and President Roosevelt for the 'unconditional surrender' of the Axis powers.

However, once Mussolini was deposed on 25 July, SOE was at the centre of the final diplomacy that led to the Armistice and the surrender of the Italian forces. SOE wireless links carried all the traffic in communications between the Italian Government and General Eisenhower's headquarters. The newly released SOE agent Lieutenant Richard Mallaby worked from a small room on the top floor of the building that housed the Italian Supreme Command in Rome. Between 30 August and the announcement of the Armistice on 8 September he sent or received 70 messages. The Lieutenant reached Brindisi with the Royal Family, politicians and generals on 10 September. He was awarded an immediate Military Cross. [2]

A small SOE mission that assisted with the Armistice negotiations in Sicily landed at Brindisi with the invasion force and provided liaison with the new government of Marshal Badoglio as part of the Allied Control Commission. Lieutenant Colonel Roseberry arrived and established close relations with a former enemy: Italian Military Intelligence, the *Servizio Informazione Militare* or SIM. The Italians placed their manpower and resources at the disposition of the British and provided a stream of reliable recruits drawn from the disbanded Italian army, navy and airforce.

With the Armistice everything had changed. Italy was no longer an enemy state, but an occupied country requiring liberation as much as France, Poland or Czechoslovakia. The role of SOE was not political subversion but liaison with a spontaneous resistance movement that could eventually provide support for the advancing Allied armies.

Contacts between the Allies and the Italian Resistance were given added value by the presence of around 50,000 escaped prisoners of war in the countryside. The Milan Liberation Committee set up its own circuit to help the fugitives within two weeks of the announcement of the Armistice, telling the Allies it felt honour bound to do so 'from a humanitarian point of view and for the good name of this country.' Gradually support networks spread throughout occupied Italy and reinforced the efforts of the official British and American search and rescue agencies, MI 9 and MIS-X, and the spontaneous gestures of small groups and individuals.

In Volume V of his extensive work *The Second World War*, Winston Churchill wrote:

> 'Mussolini's bid for a fascist revival plunged Italy into the horrors of civil war. In the weeks following the September armistice officers and men of the Italian army stationed in German-occupied northern Italy and patriots from the town and countryside began to form partisan units and to operate against the Germans and their compatriots who still adhered to the Duce. Contacts were made with the Allied armies south of Rome and with the Badoglio Government. In these months the network of Italian resistance to the German occupation was created in a cruel atmosphere of civil strife, assassinations and executions. The insurgent movement in central and northern Italy here as elsewhere in occupied Europe convulsed all classes of the people.
>
> 'Not the least of their achievements was the succour and support given to our prisoners of war trapped by the Armistice in camps in northern Italy. Out of about 80,000 of these men, conspicuously clothed in battle dress, and in the main with little knowledge of the language or geography of the country, at least 10,000, mostly helped by the local population with civilian clothes, were guided to safety, thanks to the risks taken by members of the Italian Resistance and the simple people of the countryside.' [3]

Across occupied Europe aiding escaped Allied prisoners of war and downed aircrew was the earliest and purest form of resistance. In the next chapter we look at three personal accounts which are representative of the varied prisoner of war experience in Italy after the Armistice. The soldiers had been captured within 23 days of one another at the start of Rommel's great summer offensive of 1942 in the Italian North African colony of Libya.

NOTES

1. The National Archives (TNA): Public Record Office (PRO) HS 6/776 *Assistance to Italian Patriots*, 1 July 1944.
2. Christopher Woods, 'A Tale of Two Armistices,' *War, Resistance and Intelligence*, pp. 1–17.
3. Winston S Churchill, *The Second World War, Volume V, Closing the Ring*, pp. 166–67.

2
Beyond the Wire

Sergeant Oscar D'Alcorn from Glasgow was captured by the *Deutsches Afrika Korps* at Tobruk on 20 June 1942. It was two days after his twenty sixth birthday and he was serving in the First Battalion of the Sherwood Foresters. On 14 July, Oscar arrived at Brindisi in southern Italy on board the *Nino Bixio*. Five weeks later the ship was torpedoed by the British submarine *HMS Turbulent* when she was again carrying Allied prisoners of war from North Africa.

The Foresters passed through PG 85 Tuturano before spending about a year at PG 65 Altamura in Puglia. Oscar was employed in the camp's main post office. The officer in charge was Lieutenant Augusto Ricciardi who was also the senior interpreter. He was one of three pro-British Italian officers removed from the 'Generals' camp,' PG 12 Vincigliata, near Florence, after the failed escape attempt by General Richard O'Connor in September 1942. Oscar and many of the other non-commissioned officers at Altamura were moved north to Carpi on the Emilian plain in June 1943 – ahead of possible Allied invasion.

The small town, 18 kilometres north of the provincial capital of Modena, was mainly known for its fine medieval buildings and its industry of working wood shavings. PG 73 was housed in new brick-built barracks along the Via Remesina in the hamlet of Fossoli, six kilometres north of the city centre. British files reveal that on 30 June the camp held 4,793 Allied prisoners of war: 4,636 Britons, 19 Australians, 28 Indians, 37 New Zealanders and 73 South Africans. As well as 4,667 soldiers, there were 125 airmen and a solitary sailor.

Oscar recalls the events of the Armistice:

'I had only been in the camp for nine weeks when the Italians capitulated. I was not very well at the time as I had what was referred to as Italian marsh fever, a malarial type of illness. But I joined the rest of our No. 2 compound of about 800 men on the parade square in mid-morning.

'We knew that something was happening. There were rumours galore and we were waiting for an announcement. Our Senior British Officer was Regimental Sergeant Major (RSM) Jago. At about midday he told us that an armistice was being signed and that we would all be free. He advised us to remain in camp until further notice. When the armistice was official the compound concert band would play our national anthem. Meanwhile the RSM suggested that we carry on as usual, and nobody moved. Some of the men shouted for the gates to be opened straight away, but he told us that this would not happen until he was sure it was right.

'In the late afternoon I told my pals that I would have to go and lie down. Somebody could bring me the news. I was the sole occupant of a barrack room for 120 men. Darkness arrived and we had still not heard any more. I was feeling much worse, so my friends carried me to the camp hospital. As I was admitted the Medical Officer said: "Never mind, my boy, you'll be home before the week is out." In the morning he was accompanying a German medical officer round the ward! He agreed that I should stay in bed for a few days. I still felt a bit groggy when I was discharged, but I knew that I would soon be back to normal.

'Meanwhile, life in the camp hadn't altered a great deal. The Germans left us very much to our own devices, but told us that soon we would be transferred to Germany. There were many escape attempts, though none were successful. We had the satisfaction of seeing our recent warders all enjoying the confines of a nearby compound. Those who did not take an oath of allegiance to the German cause were treated very badly.

'About a fortnight after my discharge we were given one hour's notice to pack and assemble. We were marched about three or four miles to the local railway station. I wasn't very fit for this, but managed with some help from my pals. The Italian people we met *en route* were very kind to us and gave us bread and grapes – much to the anger of the German escort. We were loaded into the usual cattle trucks and began our journey in the evening. There were frequent stops and we knew we were still in Italy the next day. As soon as we got under way we began to enlarge the air vent. In a little while it was large enough for men to get through. They were held in position from the inside and released when ready. Six or seven jumped from our truck and the same thing was happening the length of the train. I told my long-term pal that he could go too if he wanted, but he refused, as he knew that I was unfit.

'We were taken off the train the next day and had a short march to the infamous Markt Pongau transit camp in Austria. [1] Within a fortnight my friend was sent with 40 others to an *arbeitskommando*. [2] Soon afterwards, I went to an NCO camp at Spittal an der Drau where I wintered. My last year of POW life was at an *arbeitskommando* at Schladming. I was never in Germany and I am thankful for that.'

In December 1943, the camp at Carpi became the provincial detention centre for Jews, who were held under new laws. In January 1944, it evolved into the main Italian SS transit camp or *Dulag*. Political and racial prisoners were sent to concentration camps in Germany and the occupied lands. On the first train which left for Auschwitz in Poland on 22 February was Primo Levi. He wrote about his brief stay at the camp in his book *If This is a Man* and in the poem *Sunset at Fossoli*. In its seven months of operation, about 5,000 detainees passed through the doors of the centre, half of them Jews.

In 1973, a Memorial Museum to the Deportees was set up in the castle at Carpi, the *Palazzo dei Pio*. A 'Foundation for the Former Camp at Fossoli' was created in 1996 to remember and conserve its wartime history, including its original role as a camp for Allied prisoners of war.

Lieutenant Michael Goldingham was captured on 27 May 1942 near Bir Hacheim, together with the other 19 officers and 650 men of the 3rd Indian Motor Brigade. The officers were flown to Italy in Savoia bomber/transports. After passing through the grim camp at Bari they became the first residents of PG 21 in the mountains at Chieti.

In April 1943, the lieutenant was among a group of 70 prisoners of war entrained to another newly opened camp, the unused orphanage at Fontanellato in the province of Parma. He later described PG 49 as 'without doubt the luxury camp of Italy – excepting the Generals' camp near Florence.' In June, the officer employed his artistic skills in designing realistic looking documents for five escapers. They were successful in leaving the camp, but were recaptured and sent back within ten days. However, the fall of Mussolini and the Allied invasion of Sicily and then the Italian mainland signalled to all the prisoners that soon they would be returning home.

Michael Goldingham relates what actually happened:

> 'On 8 September we were disturbed by shouts of the population, rushing up and down the road outside, yelling "*Pace, Pace!*" At last it had come and we felt a pleasant thrill of anticipation as we went to bed that night.
>
> 'Little did we, let alone the Italians, realise what misery this second act of treachery would bring upon Italy. The following day, the Commandant's scouts reported the approach of the Germans from Parma to take the camp. We therefore marched out by companies to a copse three miles away, while the Commandant and garrison stayed behind to defend the camp. He was consequently captured and, we heard, was sent to Poland.
>
> 'The Germans, arriving two hours later, destroyed the furnishings and took away or sold to the Italians our belongings and the Red Cross store. The only definite news our Information Officer gave out was landings at Genoa and other places on the north west coast and the Allies being near Rome. After two cold days we decided to try to get the BBC news first-hand. On the fifth day we located a wireless and while the BBC was optimistic, all the "authenticated" news and, of course, rumours were completely false.
>
> 'We now had these courses open to us:

(1) To go to Switzerland and probably be interned. 60 miles.
(2) To go to the hills and await further landings and news. 30 miles.
(3) To take a train or bike 'hell for leather' to the south – as yet there was no fixed line. 700 miles.
(4) To walk south to meet our advancing army and lie up till it passed.

(5)   To go to France. 150 miles.
(6)   To go to Yugoslavia. 400 miles.

'Number 3 proved correct. We chose 2 …

'We were four, all Indian Army, who stayed for six weeks in a small village near Bardi. We slept in a hay barn, and fed with six families, vying with each other in hospitality. As the Fascist Government was extinct, the *contadini* had not sent in their quota of flour and there was plenty of bread. Gnocchi, macaroni, pasta asciutta, polenta, fungi, milk, grapes, chestnuts and cheese resulted in our fattening visibly in a short time.

'During the day we helped in the fields (we could watch the main road, half a mile below, for a danger sign): hoeing potatoes, ploughing, cutting wood, collecting fungi, or bringing in the grape harvest and squashing the fruit with bare feet in a coffin shaped vat. They were happy, sunny days.

'We got on well with our hosts, and being able to draw a little, we had many female sitters. They made us realise that the term "a complexion like a peach" was not hearsay. To have put cosmetics on their cheeks would have been sacrilege.

'Our great friend was Marco, the village toper, who used to lock us in his cellar and force wine on us till we could take no more. We called wine *benzina*, saying we could not work without it. When hoeing, we put the bottle ahead of us, dug hard till level with it and flopped down with cries to our pretty companion of "Maria, *benzina*!" She produced glasses, serving us with smiles and charming courtesy, till we were ready to start again …

'After six weeks of good feeding, drinking and laughter, we were no nearer freedom. Winter was coming and unless we moved over the mountains we would be caught by the snow and be unable to move south till April. In addition, the fascists were gaining power, and prisoners were their special quarry. Only recently two officers with their 75-year-old host were taken above this village. Our hosts were in worse danger than we were and four extra mouths were a lot to feed. The BBC was misleading – every day we expected the big attack and landings – and despite our hosts' discouragement and tears, John Meares and I left for the south. Paddy Bruen, whose boots were bad, and André Willis stayed behind. We heard in July that they got recaptured going to Switzerland. [3]

'We left the Bardi area on 27 October and reached the last lap on 15 December with two day stops: one through snow on 9 November, the other for food. The distance on a map is about 480 miles, but owing to the route being in the mountains except for 20 miles, the distance on foot must have been close to 900 miles, at 20 miles per day.

'Looking back, we realise how much we owe to the *contadini*, who in only a few cases refused us help. It must be born in mind that Italy was at war, that there was a reward on our heads, and that the peasants were poor. If we had been discovered, their farms would have been burnt or the family taken to Germany.

'We had a very good trip down, never once having trouble with fascists (the Germans were not the danger). Our boots just lasted. Throughout our trip we slept in the most odd places. Being late in the year and generally in the mountains, the nights were cold, and where possible we slept with the cows, who, once the odour had been mastered, gave off welcome heat …

'On 15 December we left on our last lap, along a high range of mountains. As the nights were Arctic (several frozen bodies had been found on this range and there were many cases of bad frostbite) we had planned to go "all out" without resting above the snowline.

'Food was scarce in these parts, people scared of spies, and kow-towing to the Germans. In the final village no house would give help and we had to break into a barn of shrub-wood for the night.

'The next day, resting after a steep climb, we were caught by a patrol, lead by some forest guards and woodsmen. The Germans told us they had been watching us through field glasses and followed our snow trail. We maintain that the previous day the Germans had been warned about our progress by a farmer from whom we asked water. Taken to Pescasseroli, we soon left for Opi, again being given away by an Italian when trying to escape, and so to Frosinone, where we stayed a month.'

On 4 January 1944, Lieutenant Goldingham and Captain Meares began the railway journey shared by many of their companions from Fontanellato: to the camps at Moosburg in southern Germany, Mährisch Trübau in Moravia (now the Czech town of Moravska Trebova) and lastly Brunswick in northern Germany. Final liberation came on 12 April 1945.

Private Victor Ernest Walker from Battersea in London was captured by the Germans at Gazala on 2 June 1942 while serving with 157 Field Regiment Royal Artillery. At the time of the Armistice he was based at a work camp near Novara in northern Italy, toiling all day in the rice fields on a nearby farm.

Victor recalls subsequent events:

> 'On 9 September 1943, a local girl who worked on the rice farm came running out shouting: "*Tedeschi, Tedeschi*, the Germans are coming!" I immediately put my boots on and ran into the maize fields, which at this time of year were very tall and thick. I came to a stream. Some of the prisoners jumped across, but I fell in and lay under a bush. I heard the German soldiers firing on the prisoners and saw some of them go down, but did not know if they had been shot or not. I stayed under the bush all night and then proceeded upstream. I cannot be sure of the exact number of days I walked the stream, somewhere between two to four days. I was tired, hungry, cold and feeling very bewildered. I came to a road over the stream and was prepared to give myself up to the Germans.
>
> 'I managed to scramble onto the road and saw a hay cart coming towards me with two men on it. I put my hands up in the air to surrender. The pair were Mario Baldi and his son Domenico. They turned out to be farmers from Galliate. I tried to explain to them that I was an escaped prisoner of war and that I wished to give myself up. The Italians did not understand at first, as I could not speak much Italian. After a time they seemed to understand and beckoned to me to get under the hay in the cart. They covered me over and took me to their home.'

Victor had caught malaria and was nursed by Mario and his wife Perena. The Englishman was provided with a cap, coat and trousers to conceal his fair hair and appearance. The couple told their friends that he was a disbanded Italian soldier.

When his health improved, Victor was given a bicycle and went to work on the land. He dug and ploughed alongside two Sicilian soldiers cut off in the north by the Armistice, and Domenico, who had served with the fire service in Rome and was also wanted by the fascists. The fugitives lived in another small house on the farm, which had a secret room and a large pipe through one wall to allow a quick escape into the fields. Mario and Perena brought food for the men and washed their clothes. Victor was able to go into the village and even to the cinema with Domenico, but became very anxious when he realised that most of the audience were German and Italian troops.

The Baldi family were being watched by the fascists who suspected them of sheltering prisoners of war from the camp. On 16 September, Victor and Mario were in the countryside helping Domenico look for another English prisoner of war he had met a few days earlier. Domenico left his companions, but after a few minutes they heard him cry out. He had bumped into a group of fascists with shotguns and a dog. Domenico ran off pursued by the animal and he fired a pistol shot at it. One of the militiamen caught up with the farmer and beat him to the ground. Another fascist aimed his pistol at Domenico's head and pulled the trigger. He managed to dodge the shot, but was left with a wounded hand. In the meantime, Mario arrived on the scene and scattered the enemy with musket fire, saving his son's life. As a result of this incident the fascists were on the trail of the three men. During the following week they decided to leave Galliate to join the partisans in the mountains.

Mario Baldi's wife and daughter remained in the village. However, a few days later their ration card was confiscated. One evening the Blackshirts raided the house, but the two women had already fled. They lived in the countryside for two months. Their dwelling was looted and raised to the ground by the fascists.

After leaving Galliate, Victor, Mario and Domenico walked to Lake Orta, took a boat and landed at Ronco on the western shore. They joined Captain Filippo Beltrami's partisans in the mountains above Quarna. Victor was given a rifle, a bandoleer and ammunition, and a supply of hand grenades. The band subsequently united with another formation in the Strona Valley led by two officer brothers, Alfredo and Antonio Di Dio, to form the *Brigata Patrioti Valstrona*. Their base was Campello Monti, 1,300 metres high in the mountains.

Conditions were harsh. Often the only drink was melting snow and food was a spoonful of sugar a day and anything that could be scavenged from Alpine huts that were abandoned in winter.

On 1 November, Victor was part of a detachment which marched over the mountains to Lake Maggiore and attacked a small fort at Gravellona Toce. They stormed the army barracks and took all the rifles and ammunition. In December, the partisans returned to the Lake Orta area and raided another ammunition depot at Pogno.

Later in the winter, the guerrillas moved into the Ossola Valley. Trekking over snow-covered peaks they reached Malesco, where they fought another battle with the Germans. The enemy had encircled the base of the mountain. To escape their clutches Victor's group had to flee over rough tracks and through snow and ice until they reached Craveggia in the Vigezzo Valley.

During the second week of April 1944 a scout found a suitable route to Switzerland over the Spluga Pass. A group of seven partisans including Victor and Domenico approached a Swiss frontier guard. He contacted his officer by telephone who said that Victor could enter the country, but that his companions could not.

Victor recalls:

> 'I said I would go back with them, but they pleaded with me to think of my mother. The sentry took their ammunition from them and they went away. I think the idea was in case they used it to force their way in. I was escorted to the officer who spoke English. He asked if I would like some coffee and a cigarette. I could not believe my eyes after so long without a proper drink. I was taken to a place where all my hair was shorn off and I was given a decent uniform to wear. My particulars were taken and I was informed that my name would be broadcast as being safe and well.' [4]

NOTES

1. Markt Pongau is now known as Sankt Johann im Pongau.
2. *Arbeitskommando* = work detachment.
3. Lieutenant Willis is listed in my book *British Prisoners of War in Italy: Paths to Freedom* among the escapees helped by my mother and grandparents.
4. Victor was allowed to take casual employment in Switzerland. While working on a farm at Elgg he received a letter that told him that both Mario and Domenico Baldi had managed to cross the border. The prisoners of war in the Confederation were all repatriated following the Allied invasion of southern France in August 1944. After the war, Victor was awarded a medal and two diplomas by the partisans.

3
Maryland

After the Armistice, SOE operated in Italy under the cover name of No. 1 Special Force. A new advance base was created in Puglia codenamed Maryland. It was merely intended as an out-station to handle the practical side of operations in Italy for SOE Algiers, or Massingham, but proved so useful that eventually ties with its parent were severed. A para-naval unit was sent forward at the same time to Corsica, known as Balaclava. It was headed by Captain Andrew Croft.

Maryland was led by Lieutenant Commander Gerard (Gerry) Holdsworth, RNVR, who had previously served with distinction in D Section and also in SOE's small private navy.

He recalled:

> 'After a diligent search we chose Monopoli as our headquarters – a small port halfway between Bari and Brindisi which proved to be immensely suitable, especially for our signals station which rapidly became of paramount importance.
>
> 'A parachute training establishment, a packing station both for "stores" and "chutes", and, of course, a paramilitary school were also set up on suitable terrain nearer to Bari … From these slender beginnings No. 1 Special Force became a well-organised and much respected – if not respectable – unit.'

Within four months, more than 100 agents were being trained at the school. The operations officer was Major Charles Macintosh. He had been born of New Zealand parents in Uruguay and was working for Shell Oil in Venezuela at the start of the war. Macintosh volunteered to leave his reserved occupation and in February 1941 was posted to the Inter Services Research Bureau in London, a cover name for SOE. He recounted in his book *From Cloak to Dagger* that Special Force had to overcome 'the lack of recognition by most of those in the armed forces of the possibilities offered by the Resistance movement and of the use to be made of the Italian Armed Forces that had come over to the Allied side.' [1] Gerard Holdsworth arranged a visit by the Commander-in-Chief Harold Alexander and his aide General Harding. The newly appointed SOE commander Major General Colin Gubbins also made occasional calls, given added interest by the fact that his elder son, Michael, was serving as a captain with Special Force.

By March 1944, Maryland was responsible for virtually all British special operations in Italy under the supervision of 15th Army Group and Mr Harold Macmillan, the resident Minister of State and future Prime Minister. Baker Street's influence was remote and its involvement mainly confined to coordination and logistics. Lieutenant Colonel Roseberry was withdrawn to London and created Regional Director for Italy and Switzerland.

Maryland engaged in long-term infiltration. By the end of October 1943 there were already six missions in enemy-occupied territory: one in Rome, which we will look at shortly, and the others in the north west. Three were to a Genoese surgeon called Doctor Balduzzi. Over six months his 'Otto' organisation grew rapidly and provided the Allies with valuable intelligence and assistance to escaped POWs. However, in March 1944 the fascists arrested many of the leaders and the network collapsed. Meanwhile, Special Force had set up another circuit known as *la Franchi* with the help of a Piedmont count, Edgardo Sogno, who spoke good English. An army lieutenant, he was a fervent monarchist and represented the right-wing Liberal Party on the regional military command and later on the central committee in Milan. The officer visited John McCaffery in Berne on several occasions and became his firm friend. Brave to the point of recklessness, Edgardo Sogno led his group of Green Flames in many daring missions, which eventually earned him the Italian Gold Medal for Military Valour.

Special Force also undertook paramilitary operations in support of 5th Army. In July 1943, five Anglo-Italian teams had arrived in Sicily with the invasion force. Brow Mission was led by Major Malcolm Munthe, son of the author of *The Story of San Michele*: the Swedish physician Axel

Munthe. The detachment took part in the Salerno landings and began mainland operations under the new name of Vigilant. A sea base was developed on Capri. One of its Italian motor torpedo boats was used to pluck the anti-fascist philosopher Benedetto Croce from his villa in Sorrento under the noses of the Germans. A naval facility and a training school were also established on the island of Ischia. Most of the Italian recruits were obtained through the anti-fascist political parties. After the Allies took Naples on 1 October, a headquarters was created at the Villino Salve in the Vomero district. Over four months, Vigilant mounted 70 operations, running agents in and out of enemy-held territory and aiding MI 9 in its work of rescuing escaped Allied POWs.

In January 1944, part of the task force was detached as the forward element for the entry into Rome. On the 23rd, Major Munthe and captains Michael Gubbins and Max Salvadori and their signalmen and drivers joined the Anzio beachhead. On 6 February, Major Munthe decided to reconnoitre a route to the capital which would enable the party to make direct contact with the Resistance. Captain Gubbins insisted on accompanying his friend as only he had studied the way in detail. As they reached no-man's-land they were caught by machine gun fire and narrowly managed to reach a slit trench. It was hit by a mortar shell. Major Munthe was severely wounded and Captain Gubbins was killed instantly.

When the assault on Rome became a reality in the summer, SOE wireless links proved crucial, providing the only means of communication between the Italian Government and its supporters. As 5th Army made its final attack, 11 Special Force raiding parties, totalling 48 men, provided tactical support.

Major Macintosh accompanied forward troops in their unopposed entry to the capital on 4 June. It was time to contact friends cut off for the last nine months within the British organisation for assisting Allied escaped prisoners of war. A building was taken over for a Special Force headquarters. It was swamped by a sea of administrative work in the absence of any civil administration in the city. The Major made a reconnaissance to the front line in the northern surrounds. He saw that the German defences were too strong for the infiltration of couriers and advised base that they would have to continue with sea and parachute drops.

As the Germans began a gradual retreat, partisans in the mountains were signalled to attack 16 road and rail targets. Railway lines were also sabotaged around Arezzo to aid the advance of 8th Army. In July, as Polish troops assaulted Ancona, Special Force parties hit supply columns on the coast road to the north. Electricity supplies were targeted across the area, reducing output by a half. An operation known as anti-scorch was also carried out, to prevent the Germans from destroying communications, electric power stations and factories as they retreated.

In the three months from June to August 1944, German intelligence estimated that 30,000 of their troops were killed, captured or missing as the result of partisan activity. The German Commander-in-Chief Kesselring ordered that the 'severest methods' should be taken against the guerrillas and that every violent action must be punished immediately by reprisals against civilians.

The partisans occupied Siena on 3 July, just ahead of 5th Army. In February 1945 the city provided the new base for both Maryland and Headquarters Special Operations Mediterranean.

The next target was Florence, the gateway to the Apennines. On 4 August 1944, Major Macintosh reached Canadian troops on the southern outskirts of the city in a scout car and went to partisan-held territory on the banks of the River Arno. An Italian lieutenant called Enrico Fischer arrived the following day on a mission from the Resistance in the German-occupied north. He had used a secret passage that leads through the Uffizzi Gallery to the Ponte Vecchio which the Germans had spared. The officer went back with a field telephone and 500 yards of line. A few hours later, Major Macintosh's telephone rang and he was able to speak to partisan commanders hiding in the SS headquarters in the Palazzo Vecchio across the river. The Allies were given priceless information on enemy dispositions, collected by a 70-strong partisan intelligence team.

On 6 August, the Tuscan partisan commander, Colonel Nello Niccoli, and a member of the liberation committee came across with Fischer to speak with the Major. He later made the journey himself to see whether the bridge could be used to mount an Allied attack in brigade strength, but discovered that the approaches were far too exposed. However, on the day of the rising, 11 August, the mission used the secret route to cross the river. The battle for Greater Florence lasted from 4-30 August and saw savage fighting between partisans and Germans, with limited support on the Allied side from the 21st Indian Brigade and a small number of British and Canadian troops.

In early November, a tactical headquarters (TAC HQ) was created under Major Macintosh's leadership, based in a villa between Florence and

Fiesole. The unit was attached to 5th Army to give assistance and advice on all matters concerning the control, support and employment of the Resistance in enemy-occupied territory. Special Force was to provide bombing targets and intelligence to the army and to organise courier services through the lines. The headquarters was given operational control of missions within the area, including all direct signals communications and supplies. A wireless net was also developed to provide three-way traffic between the missions, TAC HQ and Monopoli. At the end of December, a similar liaison unit was attached to 8th Army under Captain ER McDermott.

By mid-January 1945, the Apennines had been split into six tactical zones, each with a team of British and Italian officers reporting to the new headquarters. In March, the estimated partisan strength was 23,000 men. Other missions in the cities of Parma, Reggio and Modena, and elsewhere in the north, remained under the control of No. 1 Special Force base.

The Special Force commanders on the 5th Army front were given orders to strengthen their own organisations and those of the partisan formations, to stock up on supplies, and to engage only in sabotage that would not result in a major reaction by the Germans. The main priority was to be the provision of intelligence. A network of partisan observers reported on the movement and identification of enemy units, supported by the careful interrogation of prisoners. In the cities, bakeries and laundries were especially useful sources of information. The names of German officers in the 29th and 90th Panzer Grenadier divisions were known down to regimental level.

Special Force units were reconstituted as mobile teams to accompany the leading troops in jeeps and scout cars during the final offensive. As well as the tactical work with the armies during their advance, the role of Special Force in liberated territory was to establish Report Centres for mission personnel in the principal cities. The agents advised the local liberation committees on the restoration of order and the maintenance of public services until the arrival of the Allied Military Government, and then placed themselves at the disposition of the military authorities. The process of liberation went smoothly in most areas. A British company commander of the 78th Infantry Division recalled:

> 'We got across the River Po and all the way along the route it was lined by cheering Italians. It was the nearest I had ever been to being a king. There I was on my jeep and the girls would come up and kiss you and

bring you flowers and wine. This was a very great difficulty because we had to prevent the troops from taking all the wine that was offered.'

Major Charles Macintosh went forward with the troops to Bologna and on to Milan. His friend, Commander Gerard Holdsworth, DSO, had already relinquished command in Siena. On 15 January 1946 the Special Operations Executive was dissolved, its special operations role being assumed by a department of the Secret Intelligence Service.

What was it like to be a Special Force secret agent? In 1987, Max Salvadori, the senior liaison officer with the central liberation committee in Milan, told a commemorative conference at Bologna University:

'Partisan urban guerrillas and CLN members in 1943–45, as well as Italian writers on the resistance ever since, have generally ignored the difficulties SOE had in establishing contacts and sending supplies. Academic scholars and armchair strategists should try to figure out step by step how action takes place. It was not easy to cross a battlefront, whatever the means employed. A wireless set was not a bundle one could put under one's coat. In enemy territory it was not easy to find the people one was looking for, to find localities where supplies could be landed or dropped. It is easy to talk about destroying an enemy ammunition dump or bridge, it was difficult to do it. It was not easy to avoid the enemy, his collaborators and informers, to be aware of the duplicity of turncoats more interested in their factional goals than in winning the war, to recognise spies and double agents …

'Instructions given to British Liaison Officers (BLOs) were summarised in eleven words: "find who needs what and will make good use of it." In all countries in which SOE operated the BLO had to be a good judge of men, to distinguish between *attendisti* and *attivisti*, between those who would use the armament received and those who would store it: he had to endure loneliness, hunger and whatever the sky brought: he had to find his way in an unfamiliar maze. Not easy tasks. "Men and women … alone or in small numbers, deep inside enemy-held territory, giving aid to the indigenous resistance movements, and nearly always on the run." This is how *The Economist* of 16 February 1985 described SOE officers and NCOs. Wirelesses failed, drops went astray. Errors made in France, Greece, the Netherlands, Yugoslavia had to be avoided. Courage was not enough. Once behind enemy lines the BLO was no longer an officer carrying out orders: he had no other guide than himself, his sense of duty and his perception of the situation.

'At HQ not all requests could be satisfied. After the opening of two fronts in France and the changed attitude of Yugoslav partisans towards the Allies, the Italian front became less than secondary. There was scarcity of everything from DC-3s to Sten guns to blankets. In November 1944 scarcity had reached the point that led the Commander-in-Chief, desirous of avoiding the tragedy that had befallen the Polish Home Army a few weeks earlier, to warn partisans of the difficult months ahead. Scrounging, No. 1 Special Force CO was able to keep the flow of supplies at a decent level.

'What could be done, what – notwithstanding the difficulties – had to be done, was done. We did our best – always less than one wants, and often less than others expect. SOE officers died, and no publicity was given to their deaths. Others were wounded or captured. There were three operative officers when we went to Anzio. One died and one was badly wounded and never recovered. [2] There were again three when we were parachuted early in February 1945, on my way to Milan: two died. [3] The war was won and this is what matters. Members of dozens of missions sent into enemy territory did better than any armchair expert in the armed resistance of 1943-45 would have done.' [4].

NOTES

1. Charles Macintosh, DSO, *From Cloak to Dagger*, p. 29.
2. Captain Michael Gubbins and Major Malcolm Munthe. See above.
3. Major Adrian Hope of the South African Staff Corps and Captain John Keany, Royal Irish Fusiliers. Chariton Mission.
4. Max Salvadori, DSO, MC, 'Random Considerations on the Road to the CLNAI,' *No. 1 Special Force and Italian Resistance*, pp. 97–9.

4
The Italian Resistance

On 9 September 1943, as German troops secured Rome, the leaders of the anti-fascist parties met in a house on Via Adda to form the clandestine National Liberation Committee, the *Comitato di Liberazione Nazionale* or CLN. Six groups were represented: actionists, christian democrats, communists, democrats, liberals and socialists. Ivanoe Bonomi, briefly Prime Minister before Mussolini's seizure of power, was elected president.

On 16 October, the CLN issued its manifesto:

(1) To assume the constitutional powers of the state.
(2) To carry on the war alongside the Allies.
(3) To consult the people on the future form of government at the end of hostilities.

Gradually, satellite liberation committees were created in every region and province of occupied Italy. In January 1944, a central committee for northern Italy was established in Milan: the *CLN Alt Italia* or CLNAI. Its first policy statement was strongly anti-monarchist, saying: 'There will be no place tomorrow among us for a reactionary regime.' The committee informed the Allies they intended to take territory back from the Germans and wanted to be treated as the rightful government, independent of the royalist administration in the south.

Meanwhile, the number of Italians who took to the mountains to wage guerrilla warfare grew steadily. The first bands developed as a spontaneous local reaction to the German takeover. The leaders were mainly traditional anti-fascists and disbanded Italian officers. In the winter of 1943 there were probably 10,000 partisans. This figure had trebled by spring 1944 and reached 80,000 by early summer. At the start of 1945, there were about 130,000 guerrillas.

Max Salvadori, the senior SOE liaison officer with the CLNAI, wrote that the willingness of an unexpected number of Italians to take up arms against the Germans and their collaborators was a development which most people in Italy and outside had not foreseen:

> 'Guerrilla warfare is even more cruel than conventional war, the chances of surviving slimmer. Whoever joined a patriot or partisan band ... signed his or her death warrant. "It had to be seen to be believed," was said later. It was the atonement for fascist crimes.' [1]

The partisan network was highly politicised: 40 to 50 per cent of the fighters belonged to communist formations, the Garibaldi brigades. After 20 years of underground activity, and military experience in the Spanish Civil War, the party was organised and motivated for the struggle ahead. With a membership of only a few thousand in September 1943, the Garibaldini were still able to gain ascendancy over the Resistance, though they never enjoyed the military monopoly of the party in Albania, Greece and Yugoslavia.

Another 30 per cent of the partisans were enrolled in the Justice and Liberty (*Giustizia e Libertà* or GL) brigades of the Action Party. The remainder were usually socialist – the Matteotti brigades – liberal or Catholic. There were also some avowedly non-political formations, the *Autonomi*, which had been created by regular army officers. After the Badoglio Government declared war on Germany on 13 October 1943, all those who felt bound by their oath of loyalty to the King found themselves free to disobey the fascist republic. Sometimes also known as Green Flames, the independent units were usually strongly monarchist and eager to cooperate with the Allies.

Allied contact with the Resistance was opened through Switzerland in the winter of 1943. The initial meeting was held in Lugano on 3 November. John McCaffery, the SOE head, held discussions with two non-communist representatives: Alfredo Pizzoni and Ferruccio Parri. Pizzoni was a decorated war hero and Milanese banker who became independent president of the CLNAI and also took on responsibility for obtaining the necessary finances for the Resistance. Parri was a founder member of the Action Party in 1942 and leader of the GL partisan formations. The Italians were promised money and supplies. Fifty million lire were sent, but the British Foreign Office intervened to ensure that only limited supplies and a handful of agents were dropped. The first airlift was made on 23 December and provided equipment for merely 30 men. The CLN complained bitterly, saying that the Allies were defaulting on their promises and wanted random acts of sabotage rather than widespread resistance.

Winston Churchill and the Foreign Office viewed the Italian Resistance as too republican, too left wing and too communist. The War Office also disliked irregulars. The Allies, particularly the British, supported the monarchy as the guarantor of political stability, while the CLN argued that King Vittorio Emanuele III had *de facto* abdicated by fleeing Rome with his government and generals on 9 September 1943. At a congress of anti-fascist parties held at Bari in January 1944, the left-wingers led by the CLN were unanimous in demanding the king's immediate abdication.

Help in bridging the gap between the Allies and the Italian Resistance, and between the anti-fascists in the north and south, came from a most unlikely quarter: the communist leader Palmiro Togliatti who returned after 18 years of exile. Togliatti was aware that there was no possibility of revolution in a country emerging from 20 years of fascism and occupied by the Allies. So he announced the abandonment of revolutionary action in favour of national unity, progressive democracy and permanent coalition of the popular parties. Togliatti told his National Council:

> 'It is impossible to give any guarantee of freedom to the Italian people until the Nazis have been driven from our native soil. We must therefore redouble our war effort in order to liberate our country. Let us, then, form a national government. In doing so we shall be taking an immense step forward.'

The anti-fascist parties accepted a plan whereby King Vittorio Emanuele would hand over his powers to his son, Crown Prince Umberto, who would be created Lieutenant General on the day the Allies entered Rome. A coalition government was formed under Marshal Badoglio on 24 April. Following the liberation of the capital on 4 June, the government of the south ceased to exist and Ivanoe Bonomi replaced Badoglio as leader of a new government in Rome. The principle of national coalition was maintained in the ministry, which declared itself the expression of the Committee of National Liberation.

The CLNAI approved the formation of the Rome government and in the summer there was a noticeable increase in Allied moral support and material aid for the Resistance.

On 9 June 1944, a central military command for occupied Italy was established in Milan under the banner of the Corps of Volunteers for Liberty, the *Corpo Volontari della Libertà* or CVL. The five main parties were represented: actionists, Christian democrats, communists, liberals and socialists, though the committee was inspired by the communist example and was dominated by the commander of its Garibaldini formations, Luigi Longo, and by Ferruccio Parri, leader of the GL brigades.

Soon the concept of a military committee affiliated to the CLN, but working independently of it, was extended across occupied Italy. A vertical chain of command was created, running from the central CVL committee to regional and provincial bodies. They in turn directed divisions, the operational units, which were composed of two or more brigades, the tactical formations. The days of isolated partisan bands consisting of 30 or so men were over.

In August, General Raffaele Cadorna was parachuted into the Val Cavallina, east of Bergamo, to become supreme commander in the north. The officer belonged to Italy's most distinguished military family and had valiantly opposed the German occupation of Rome as commander of the *Ariete* armoured division. General Cadorna was accompanied by an SOE liaison officer, Major Oliver Churchill, and a wireless operator. The General told the CLNAI that they could rely on money and supplies from the Allies, but that aid would be suspended if operations were impeded by political disagreements. The communists opposed the General's appointment, saying it overrode the claims of their leader, Luigi Longo. A compromise was reached in November after British intervention. General Cadorna was nominated as partisan commander, with Longo and Parri as his joint chiefs of staff, though it was February 1945 before the appointment was finally approved.

In the field, disagreements between the communists and the other partisan groups were also frequent, usually over the allocation of supplies. The historian of the Italian Resistance, Roberto Battaglia, himself a former GL partisan and SOE operative, wrote:

> 'Equipment and ammunition were forthcoming from the Allies, but unfortunately they acted so cautiously, showed so much political discrimination, that they almost invariably stirred up disputes between the various partisan formations.
>
> 'The Allied missions behind the lines gave precedence to the groups that leaned towards the right, believing that these would afford them the greatest support, but even so, they were strangely inconsistent and were actuated on the whole by personal preference. In Piedmont, for example, they supplied arms to the Autonomi and refused help to the GL and Garibaldi formations. In Liguria, they provided the GL with what they required, but did not assist the Garibaldini, while in Emilia they furnished the Garibaldini with supplies, possibly because they had practically no other alternative!' [2]

Max Salvadori reveals the origin of many of these problems:

> 'Guerrilla groups and the smaller units in towns had usually been the result of the initiative of one individual, or at most a few, from the confidence a leader inspired and his ability not only as a commander but also in solving particular logistical problems. Small groups being the basic operative unit, it had been right to send BLOs to liase with specific ones. This also had its drawbacks: it was often interpreted as playing favourites. The group receiving supplies tended not to share them with others and the BLO easily identified himself with the group to which he was attached and ignored the others.
>
> 'As for the political arm of the Resistance, the BLO's position was often made difficult by lack of familiarity with a complex situation in which forces that had no counterpart in Allied nations played a significant role and by ignorance of the background and position of leading CLN figures. Many members of the CLN and of its military committees were no newcomers. Besides being courageous, many of them had a most distinguished record, politically, and also militarily in World War I or the Spanish Civil War. They were exceptional people of considerable intellectual and moral stature. They formed the backbone of the Resistance, they were its mind and conscience.' [3]

Professor Mackenzie neatly summarises the opposition structures that had evolved at local level:

> 'The six parties – Liberal, Democrat, Action Party, Christian Democrat, Socialist, Communist – became recognisable as formed bodies, with

leaders and principles and clandestine newspapers. In spite of divisions and cross-divisions as regards the monarchy, religion, property and almost everything else, there arose in most towns a Committee of National Liberation (CLN) representing all the parties, backed by a Corps of Volunteers of Freedom (CVL) which included all active fighting elements irrespective of party affiliation.

'The general pattern of activity was that in the mountains there would be bands of deserters, fugitives from fascist conscription, "broken men" of all kinds, quietly but warmly supported by the peasantry, poorly armed, but on the whole good fighting material. Among them were a surprising number of escaped Allied prisoners of a variety of colours, creeds and nations.

'Each major town would have a circle of active politicians, who combined mutual suspicion with mutual support, and exercised a rather shadowy collective influence over the partisans in the mountains. The latter were dependent on the towns for many things – money, forged papers, information on enemy movements, technical supplies of many kinds, sometimes even for food.' [4]

In the cities, groups and squads also emerged dedicated to guerrilla warfare, recruitment and propaganda: *Gruppi d'Azione Patriottica* or GAP and *Squadre d'Azione Partigiana* or SAP.

Women played an active part in the clandestine movement, sometimes as fighters, but more often as couriers or despatch riders, known as *staffette*, and providers of sanctuary to partisans and to Allied escaped prisoners, downed aircrew and special forces.

On 30 June 1944, a revealing report was circulated by the Republican Army Headquarters giving its explanation for the expansion of the Resistance:

> 'The majority of the population shows itself largely sympathetic towards the rebels for the following reasons:
> (1) The general aversion to fascism and the consequent growth of dissatisfaction.
> (2) Antipathy towards the Germans.
> (3) The widespread desire for the war to be brought to an end as soon as possible and by whatever means are possible.
> (4) The call up of the 1921, 1922 and 1926 age groups, which afforded the rebels the opportunity for much useful propaganda.

(5) The comparative failure of the mopping-up campaign. The measures taken were not sufficiently stringent, nor were the forces at our disposal adequate in number.
(6) The irregular conduct of certain of the personnel engaged in this campaign, which showed up the National Republican Guard in a very unfavourable light, and was another valuable source of rebel propaganda.
(7) The failure of the authorities to maintain strict surveillance over the population, in particular, the population of the valleys.
(8) The removal by the Germans of machinery from certain factories for use elsewhere and the fear of being deported to Germany have provoked widespread strikes and have induced the working class, as well as other sections of the community, to give more or less open support to the rebels.'

In his *History of the Italian People*, Giuliano Procacci wrote of the partisan summer:

'The liberation of Rome and of Florence in June and August 1944 respectively, and the imminent prospect of a final Allied victory certainly did much to intensify the activity of partisan formations organised by the various parties in the north. Lightning attacks and acts of sabotage multiplied and various "free zones" were constituted, entirely occupied and administered by the partisans, such as the Val d'Ossola, Carnia, the republic of Torriglia in Liguria, and others besides.

'The subsequent course of events showed moreover that the Italian Resistance was not an ephemeral phenomenon, and that it in no way intended to confine itself to the position of a body of snipers and saboteurs supplementary to the Allied armies, as the Allies, worried by the political implications of the Resistance, would have liked it to be.' [5]

At the end of the summer, the Allied assault on the Gothic Line ground to a halt. The Germans and fascists brought up five divisions and auxiliary formations to take on the partisans who had launched an all-out offensive on Allied instructions. The guerrillas were forced to take up defensive positions in the hope of preventing the liberated zones in Emilia, Liguria, Lombardy, Piedmont and the Veneto from being overrun.

On 10 November, General Alexander issued his controversial declaration to the Resistance. In a radio message the partisans were told that the

Allies were unable to launch their final offensive until the spring. Deteriorating weather conditions had prevented the northward drive. As a result the fighters should:

(1) Cease for the present from engaging in any large-scale operations.
(2) Conserve all stores of ammunition and await further orders.
(3) Listen in whenever possible to the broadcasts of *Italia Combattente* transmitted from Allied HQ in order to keep in touch with any changes that might occur in the situation and to be in readiness to act on new directives.

Though intended to save unnecessary loss of life, the declaration was a great setback for the Resistance. On the other hand, it was a tonic for the Germans and Republicans. With the guarantee that they would not be liable to major attack over the winter, they unleashed a series of offensives in the mountains, adopting the tactic of the *rastrellamento* or round up: armoured columns penetrated the valleys, with supporting infantry deployed on the hills, while further units scoured the secondary valleys. At the same time, there was increased police activity in the cities. The military commands of Liguria, Lombardy, Piedmont and the Veneto were arrested. In January 1945, Ferruccio Parri was detained and Lieutenant Sogno captured in a failed attempt to rescue him – a gesture symbolic of the new unity of the Resistance

Giuliani Procacci wrote of this period:

> 'The ten months from September 1944, when the Allied troops were held on the Gothic Line, to April 1945, when northern Italy was liberated, were very hard months for the partisan movement. To this period belong the most massive German manhunts and the most pitiless reprisals against the civilian population. The most terrible of all of these was probably that inflicted on the commune of Marzabotto in Emilia where 1,830 people were killed. The Germans reoccupied many free zones and it was during this period that most of the 46,000 dead of the war of liberation lost their lives.' [6]

On 2 December 1944, the CLNAI gave its response to the Alexander proclamation in a document drafted by the communist Luigi Longo. He stated:

> 'The partisan war is not on the part of the Italian people and the patriots who have taken up arms a mere whim, an idle caprice to be

refrained from at will … the war must go on. There must be no relaxation, no weakening. On the contrary the struggle must be intensified, the armed forces engaged in it greatly increased. We cannot, indeed, we must not, consider any suggestion calculated to deflect us from our purpose: that of widening the sphere of our activities, bringing still larger numbers into the field, and fighting on with an ever growing resolution and will to win.'

The lack of coordination between the Allies and the Resistance revealed by the Alexander proclamation meant that a joint plan of action was urgently required. Less than a month later the problem was partially resolved when a CLNAI mission arrived in Rome. Alfredo Pizzoni led the delegation, supported by Ferruccio Parri, Giancarlo Pajetta, Longo's deputy, and Edgardo Sogno. After discussions with the Italian Government and the Allied Forces Headquarters (AFHQ) at Caserta, the 'Rome Protocols' were signed by General Maitland Wilson for the Allies and by the four Resistance leaders. On 26 December, the agreement was also approved by a new Bonomi government, now composed of only three parties: Christian democrats, communists and liberals.

As a result of the agreements:

(1) The Italian government 'delegated the CLNAI to represent it in the struggle' in occupied Italy.
(2) The CLNAI accepted the Italian government as the legitimate authority in the rest of Italy.
(3) The CLNAI agreed to accept the military directives of General Alexander and to nominate a commander who would be acceptable to both sides as head of the CVL. The choice fell on General Cadorna.

The CLNAI also undertook that once the north was liberated they would hand over their powers to the Allied Military Government (AMG), disband the partisan formations and surrender their weapons. The Allies agreed to pay a subsidy of 160 million lire a month to the Resistance from money donated by the Italian Government as their contribution to the war effort. Alfredo Pizzoni signed the financial accord at Caserta and became responsible for the transfer of the funds and their distribution in the north. The currency was allocated in the ratio of 40 per cent to the Garibaldi brigades and 60 per cent to other partisan groups.

Despite these carefully drafted agreements, the Allies became increasingly uneasy about the direction of Italian politics as the final offensive loomed. The British Foreign Office continued to highlight the communist menace and insisted that AFHQ should adopt a new attitude towards the partisans.

Accordingly, Professor Mackenzie wrote, over the winter:

> 'The idea of relatively large partisan forces was abandoned: the Italian role would no longer be to eke out the slender Allied strength by a sustained guerrilla offensive, but to continue minor sabotage, to take steps to prevent "scorching" of Italian resources by the Germans, and to be ready to maintain order when the collapse came. This meant that military supplies to north Italy would be substantially reduced and aircraft diverted to other purposes: that liaison officers would be asked particularly to watch the political situation and keep some control of the destination of supplies: and that the main plan would not be one for armed rising but for "counter-scorch" and a peaceful takeover in what were commonly known as "Rankin" conditions – those of a German collapse or voluntary withdrawal.' [7]

What actually happened on the liberation – and the history of the Italian Resistance in general – is not widely known outside the country. As recently as 1998, a noted American OSS agent, Peter Tompkins, wrote:

> 'The contribution of Italian anti-fascist partisans to the campaign in Italy in World War II has long been neglected. These patriots kept as many as seven German divisions out of the line. They also obtained the surrender of two full German divisions, which led directly to the collapse of the German forces in and around Genoa, Turin and Milan.
>
> 'These actions pinned down the German armies and led to their complete destruction. Throughout northern Italy, partisan brigades in the mountains and clandestine action groups in the cities liberated every major city before the arrival of combat units of Fifteenth Army Group, a mixture of American, British, French and Commonwealth divisions, to which was added a smattering of royalist Italians.
>
> 'The partisans' success was largely attributable to the arms and supplies parachuted to them by the British Special Operations Executive (SOE) and the OSS and to the brilliance of the intelligence networks developed by members of the Resistance in constant touch with Fifteenth Army Group headquarters via secret radios.' [8]

The Allied airlift to the Italian Resistance is the topic of the next two chapters.

NOTES

1. Max Salvadori, DSO, MC, 'Random Considerations on the Road to the CLNAI,' *No. 1 Special Force and Italian Resistance*, p. 96.
2. Roberto Battaglia, *The Story of the Italian Resistance*, pp. 147–8.
3. Max Salvadori, DSO, MC, op. cit., p. 97.
4. WJM Mackenzie, *The Secret History of SOE*, pp. 549–50.
5. Giuliano Procacci, *History of the Italian People*, p. 451.
6. Ibid., p. 451.
7. WJM Mackenzie, op. cit., pp. 554–5.
8. Peter Tompkins, 'The OSS and Italian Partisans in World War II,' *Studies in Intelligence*, Spring 1998 edition.

5
Secret Air Missions

During the Italian campaign Allied aircraft delivered 4,469 tons of supplies to the partisans. This was achieved by no more than four special duty squadrons and a varying number of bombers and transports diverted from their usual roles. The figure represents almost 20 per cent of the cargoes dropped in the Mediterranean theatre and most of the rest was carried by aircraft flying from Italian fields.

The Allied conquest of much of southern Italy in September and October 1943 marked a turning point in the air war. All of German-occupied Europe was now within range of aircraft from Britain or Italy. The British and Americans took over Italian bases on the coast and across the Foggia plain. New airfields were also constructed by covering olive groves with gravel and perforated steel planking.

The 205 Bomber Group Royal Air Force (RAF) was formed at Foggia under the leadership of South African Major General JT Durrant. The unit was subject to the operational control of 15th United States Army Air Force (USAAF) and its night bombers complemented the American daylight force. 205 Group was organised in four wings: 231st, 236th and 240th RAF and the 2nd South African Air Force (SAAF), each composed of two squadrons. The South Africans were equipped with Consolidated Liberator B-24 VIs and the aircraft also gradually replaced the popular Wellington bombers across the rest of the group.

Alongside the bomber offensive, secret air missions began from Italy to destinations as far afield as the Balkans, Czechoslovakia and Poland, mainly using personnel, aircraft and equipment transferred from North Africa.

Fortunately, the start of the Italian airlift coincided with a new allocation of aircraft for special duties. In January 1944, the British Chiefs of Staff approved proposals to increase the number of dedicated planes in the Mediterranean to 46. Numbers 148 and 624 squadrons and the Polish flight, number 1586, formed 334 Wing RAF in Brindisi. Two American Liberator squadrons were also in training in England and extra help would be provided by No. 38 (Air Transport) Group RAF.

334 Wing was equipped with Halifax bombers and in addition the Poles had three Liberators. Short Stirling Mark IV bombers were brought into service in the summer of 1944 and Number 148 Squadron was finally given Liberator VIs. Though mainly a heavy bomber, the plane was also the leading Allied cargo transport and proved an ideal workhorse for the special duty squadrons. The Liberators were highly modified, had minimal identification markings and were painted black all over.

The 624th Squadron had returned to Algeria for operations over southern France in February 1944. The unit was disbanded in September, with some crews moving to 148 Squadron. The following February, 624 Squadron was reactivated as a mine spotting unit, flying over the Adriatic from Foggia and other bases in the Mediterranean.

Special Force also had a few aircraft under its direct control. At first these were two Italian Savoia-Marchetti SM 82 heavy bomber/transports. When a tactical headquarters (TAC HQ) was created near Florence under Major Charles Macintosh in November 1944, it co-operated with 12th USAAF in 'Lighthouse Operations' to shelter and guide downed airmen through enemy lines. In appreciation, a Mitchell B 25 light bomber was placed at the HQ's disposition. The plane set a record by delivering ammunition to partisans in a combat zone only three hours after receipt of a coded radio message.

For landings and pick ups in Italy the British generally used Lysanders and the Americans Dakotas. TAC HQ soon also obtained an Italian two-seater fighter trainer, the Nardi 305, and a German artillery observation plane, the Fieseler Storch, which suited the rough landing strips that could be improvised in the mountains. The aircraft were flown on many dangerous operations by Lieutenant Furio Lauri, one of Italy's most decorated airmen. At various times the passengers included escaped prisoners of war, downed airmen and wounded agents or partisans.

The fate of the Resistance was increasingly bound up with the ability of these aircraft to reach their targets. Air supply was usually the only practical option.

In his book *SOE*, Professor Michael Foot wrote that 'Politically-minded resisters and many post-war authors have been a little too inclined to think of parachute drops as if they were like the Lord's scattering of manna in Sinai for the people of Israel,' or, 'like rain-storms: simply events that happened from the sky.' [1] We will not make that mistake.

WJM Mackenzie compared the technical difficulties involved to 'like trying to get home in the dark to an aerodrome controlled by irresponsible amateurs,' adding that 'it was many times worse for landing operations.' [2] Special duty flights suffered a failure rate of about 1 in 3 due to enemy action, bad weather, lack of navigation aids and the non-appearance of reception parties.

The dangers were confirmed by William Pickering, MM – a wireless operator with Special Force from the Sicily landings to the liberation – who told me that three sets of landing fires greeted their Dakota during his final operation: the Chariton Mission to Piedmont. One signal was from the target site held by the *Autonomi* of Major Enrico Mauri. The other fires had been lit by the Germans as a decoy and by communist partisans hoping to receive supplies. The aircraft circled the valley for 20 minutes before the pilot was able to approve the drop.

The aircrews for secret missions were carefully selected and trained in long range navigation. The planes flew at low altitude to avoid enemy fighters, anti-aircraft defences, radar and sound detection devices. The crews became skilled in flying across mountainous terrain by night. A phase of the moon was chosen which promised clear skies and reasonable visibility. The aircraft reduced altitude to a few hundred feet and decelerated to near stall speeds of 135 miles per hour or less. On one of these missions, a B-17 Flying Fortress of the American 885th Bombardment Squadron was struck by small arms ground fire from above!

The wireless telegraph (W/T) was the crucial link in coordinating aerial and ground activities. When Italy surrendered in September 1943, an SOE signals station moved forward from Algiers to Brindisi and soon became established at Monopoli. The final location was at the Special Operations Mediterranean (SOM) headquarters in Siena. Wireless operators like William Pickering were key members of SOE missions to enemy occupied territory and most parachute drops were arranged over their sets. Proposed drop zones were carefully reviewed by the Air Force. If approved, Special Force base would allocate a codename and log the map coordinates. A list of short and simple messages authorised by the BBC was held in the safe. They were broadcast as personal messages at the end of the news on the Italian programme to indicate whether or not a mission would be carried out.

Other avenues were also available. Notice of the first airdrop to the partisans in the Arda Valley (where my family lived) was sent in May 1944 by the 'Franchi' organisation of Edgardo Sogno in Switzerland. The message alerting the group was: 'Radio Monteceneri calling. "Franchi" reports that the petrol is burning,' and confirmation of an imminent drop was given a few days later by the phrase 'The house is in ruins.' [3]

When an aircraft was over the drop zone, signals contact was made with the Resistance reception party. With the plane at a height of between 300 and 500 feet, the bomb aimer would release containers of arms and explosives from the bay, with parachutes to slow their rate of fall. The holders were metal cylinders, just over a foot in diameter and 5' 9" long, that could carry up to 100 kg, a four-man load. Gaps were filled with clothing and other scarce goods such as coffee and tobacco. Aircraft were able to carry between 12 and 18 of the canisters. A few stores like uniforms, blankets and even boots, could be thrown from the aircraft without the need for holders or wrapping.

Packages and panniers were stacked inside the plane's fuselage and released by the dispatcher through a hole a metre wide cut into the floor. Agents (nicknamed 'Joes' by the Americans) were also dropped through this opening at a height of around 600 feet. A red light turned to green, the dispatcher's arm swept down as he shouted 'Go!' and the operative launched into space, springing to attention to avoid becoming entangled with the chords of the parachute as it was pulled open by the static line.

A parachutist's departure was easier from one type of aircraft, the Douglas Dakota C-47 transporter – designated the DC-3 by the British – which was widely used by the Allies in Italy. The agent simply leaped out of a door on the port side of the plane. In his story of the Chariton Mission, *The Bandits of Cisterna*, William Pickering recalled:

> 'The red light came on and the six of us lined up. We were all wearing the Irvine Statachutes which opened automatically (or so we were assured!).
>
> 'Hope, Keany, Giovanni, Millard and Salvadori went ahead of me at one-second intervals, giving me longer than them to reflect on my

stupidity for finding myself in such a situation. Then the despatching sergeant tapped me on the shoulder. I stepped out into space and felt the icy blast of the cold night air on my exposed face.

'Before I had time to think further my 'chute had opened and I felt the welcoming tug of the harness on my shoulders. That slight pain produced a surge of relief as I realised I was not about to become a "Roman Candle."

'As I floated down I had thirty long seconds to consider my situation. I was about to land 100 miles behind enemy lines and the Germans had already lit a fire to welcome us. I looked upwards longingly at the disappearing Dakota.' [4]

Unfortunately, parachute training had overlooked snow landings and the mission fell into deep drifts. The commander, Major Max Salvadori, fondly remembered 'the efficient and enthusiastic young W/T operator Sergeant Pickering, who had dug me out of the snow while Captain Ballard, in charge of the reception committee, was shouting: "Be quick, the Germans are coming!" [5]

British liaison officers were always given instructions for the reception of supplies. A seven-point list told them to appoint an overall commander, two-man squads for each signal fire, and others made up of a commander and four men to collect containers, parachutes and free drops. Peasants with carts would be required to transport the goods to the mission stores, where the commander of each squad would hand them in to the storeman. Guards would also be needed to keep unauthorised people away.

The rules end: 'All packing lists will be brought immediately (unopened) to the British Liaison Officer. It is the responsibility of the Reception Commander to ensure that the drill is known to all his men and that it is properly carried out.'

Sometimes the drops were not so productive. The first airlift to the partisans in the Arda Valley duly arrived on 17 May 1944, but consisted of just 15 Sten guns, some packs of plastic explosive, 10 mines, a similar number of tunics, some '5s' packets of cigarettes, and outsize shoes for the left foot only. [6] A parachute drop to the International Battalion of Major Gordon Lett in the Rossano Valley in November 1944 provided bags of dried potatoes, and antique blunderbusses, nearly five foot long, with a ramrod attached to the barrel, and a beautiful embossed butt inscribed with the date 1890. [7]

As we have seen in Chapter Three, six SOE missions were already in the field by the end of October 1943. The most important was the Rudder Mission to Rome. It was led by Italian Captain Fabrizio Vassalli, who volunteered to cross enemy lines with the code to open wireless links between the partisans and the Allies. For more than five months, the officer collected intelligence and coordinated sabotage as aide to a senior Italian staff officer, Colonel Giuseppe Lanza di Montezemolo, who ran an underground military front several hundred strong.

In March 1944, the two leaders were arrested. Allied investigations following the capture of the capital on 4 June revealed that the SS had subjected them to gruelling interrogation and torture. A report by SOE recorded: 'Neither betrayed his collaborators. Had either done so the organisation would certainly have been wiped out. Both were eventually shot.' [8] Colonel di Montezemolo and Captain Vassalli were posthumously awarded the Italian Gold Medal for Military Valour.

Over the next 6 months, another 18 SOE missions were sent to occupied Italy, 41 men in all. Between June and September 1944 a further 17 teams followed, consisting of 54 operatives of whom 37 were British and 17 Italian. It was estimated that there were now almost 200 SOE agents in northern Italy, including 33 W/T operators. On the eve of the final Allied offensive in April 1945, the force had grown to 217 men: 59 British officers, 66 'other ranks' and 92 Italians.

In addition, there were many independent American missions from the Office of Strategic Services (OSS). When President Roosevelt and the Joint Chiefs of Staff were signing the orders creating the agency in June 1942, its head, Brigadier General William Donovan, was in London negotiating with SOE. The two countries agreed to cooperate in the field, with the division of theatres of operations. Italy was to be shared: OSS and SOE would run their own missions from an integrated headquarters. A senior British Liaison Officer, Lieutenant Colonel Peter McMullen, remarked later that: 'To anyone with experience of field conditions this spelt the most dire confusion.'

The 2677th Regiment OSS (Provisional) operated from Caserta with responsibility for the Mediterranean theatre. Brindisi was the base for aerial and maritime activities and the radio network was located at Bari.

Field detachments of the Special Operations branch worked with partisans along the forward zone of the Allied advance and deep within occupied Italy. The job mainly involved setting up radio links for established Resistance groups, calling in supplies, and making preparations to sabotage enemy communications and supply routes. To support these activities, the Americans added two dedicated squadrons to the bombers and transports already in use.

During the final phase of the war in Italy, Special Force estimated that the Americans would send at least as many supplies as the British since they had more aircraft. The OSS helped any group fighting the Germans and fascists whatever their politics. As a result, the Resistance was well armed during the final offensive despite British attempts to ration the flow of weapons to left-wing groups.

The Special Flight Section of the 12th USAAF had been activated in North Africa in October 1943. In September the following year, its successor, the 885th Bombardment Squadron (Heavy) (Special), moved from Algeria to Brindisi and began missions as part of 15th AAF.

The second squadron originated in the main OSS airlift into Europe, codenamed Operation Carpetbagger, which began in January 1944 from Tempsford in Bedfordshire. Twenty-four Consolidated Liberator aircraft were assigned to special duties

On 5 August, Carpetbagger missions became the responsibility of the 492nd Bombardment Group (Heavy), based at Harrington in Northamptonshire. The unit also continued in a conventional bombing role. In December one of its four squadrons, the 859th Bombardment (Heavy), flew to Brindisi to reinforce the 885th.

The two special duty squadrons formed the 15th Special Group (Provisional) under Colonel Monro MacCloskey on 20 January 1945. The 885th Squadron operated mainly in Italy and the 859th over the Balkans, but they could be employed in the same area if weather conditions made it advisable. The 885th Squadron was equipped with Liberators and Boeing B-17 Flying Fortresses, while the 859th only had Liberators.

At the peak of its operations in February, the Special Group flew half a million miles in Italy and the Balkans and dropped 34 agents and 892 tons of weapons and supplies. Seventy three per cent of the sorties were successful, 354 out of 486, with the failures nearly all due to lack of reception parties. The group was awarded a Distinguished Unit Citation for operations involving both squadrons in the Po Valley on the night of 17–18 February.

Meanwhile, Headquarters Special Operations Mediterranean and Maryland relocated to Siena. The main SOE dispatch centre moved forward from Brindisi to Malignano Airfield in Tuscany. Nearby Rosignano was also sometimes used and on 24 March it became the new home of the American unit, redesignated the 2641st Special Group (Provisional).

From January to May 1945 the American squadrons deployed 34 aircraft with 48 crews and their ground support personnel. As a result of enemy action and the hazards of special operations the group lost 7 planes and 35 airmen. In addition, several downed crew members were captured by the enemy and became prisoners of war. [9]

In the final four months of the war in Italy, Allied aircraft delivered 2,544 tons of supplies to the Resistance. This compares to 1,920 tons in the whole of 1944 and a mere 5 tons in 1943. These figures are the product of several thousand individual sorties by planes of the special duty squadrons and bombers and transports acting in a supplementary role.

The missions flown by the South African Air Force are the topic of the next chapter. Its inclusion in the book is due to my meeting the daughter of one of the airmen in London in 2002. It was at a lecture on 'Life with the Italian Partisans,' given by Sir Stephen Hastings, MC, the wartime British Liaison Officer in my family's home province of Piacenza. At the talk, Mrs Anne Storm told me the poignant story which forms the second part of the chapter.

NOTES

1. MRD Foot, *SOE*, p. 140.
2. WJM Mackenzie, *The Secret History of SOE*, p. 364.
3. Giuseppe Prati, *La Resistenza in Val d'Arda*, pp. 48–50.
4. William Pickering with Alan Hart, *The Bandits of Cisterna*, pp. 20–1.
5. Max Salvadori, 'Mission to the CLNAI,' *No. 1 Special Force and Italian Resistance*, p. 473.
6. Giuseppe Prati, op. cit., p. 50.
7. Gordon Lett, DSO, *Rossano*, p. 140.
8. TNA: PRO HS 6/818.
9. Special Group information compiled by John K Mattison, veteran of the 885th Squadron, and Hugh S Turner, nephew of Leslie L Turner, killed in action, 859th

Squadron.

6
The SAAF Liberators

On Thursday, 12 October 1944, 20 Allied heavy bombers took off on a special duty mission from Celone, one of the Foggia group of airbases. The aircraft were the Liberators of the 2nd South African wing of 205 Group RAF.

Though formed as recently as the previous April, the group's 31st and 34th squadrons were already veterans of the airlift to occupied Europe from Italy. Twelve days after the start of the Warsaw Rising, the night flying Liberators of the SAAF and 178 Squadron RAF had joined 334 Wing RAF in flights to the Polish capital, a round trip of about 2,000 miles on a zig-zag course.

The *SAAF War Diary* records a typical sortie, made in this case on 14 August 1944:

> 'Liberator KG 858 H, with Major SS Urry as pilot, departed from the airfield at Celone at 19h30 on its second flight to Warsaw. The previous night the aircraft had been forced to turn back as a result of technical problems and therefore had not been able to reach Warsaw.'

The rest of the crew on the 14th were: Lieutenants Armstrong, Collard and Metelerkamp, and Warrant Officers Bloch and Lordan, all SAAF, Sergeant Lockey, RAF, and Flying Officer Millar, Royal Australian Air Force (RAAF), Anne's father.

The Diary continues:

> 'Initially the second flight went without a hitch. One light-aircraft battery and one searchlight were noticed in the vicinity of Cracow and two light anti-aircraft batteries were observed in the vicinity of Ochota. The crew reached the Vistula approximately 11 kilometres south of

Warsaw, from where they could see red flashes and searchlights. From there the aircraft flew along the eastern bank towards the city. As a result of the smoke that enveloped the city, they could not positively identify any building. All 12 metal containers were dropped on the indicated zones. Two spotlights were observed to the east of zone A. Anti-aircraft fire was experienced over zones A, B and C. Then the aircraft was hit by a shell which caused a 15 centimetres hole in the fuselage. Problems were also experienced with the radio, the steering gear and the intercom in the front turret. During their flight over the city, they saw several Liberators being shot down, one of which crashed to the west of the target area.

'During the return flight, air-to-air firing was noticed to the left of Cracow. An aircraft that had been hit was seen to crash. Although KG 858 H had been damaged by enemy fire, which caused many problems for the pilot and his crew, it managed to reach its home base at Celone safely at 05h50 after a flight of 10 hours and 20 minutes.' [1]

Another of the pilots from 131 Squadron, Major Jack van Eyssen, DFC, recalled:

'We started to loose height and as we drew closer to the city were shocked by what we saw, in spite of having been told what to expect at the briefing. Row upon row of buildings were on fire, sending clouds of smoke thousands of feet into the air. The smoke was in turn illuminated from below by the fires. It was obvious that a life or death struggle was taking place before us.' [2]

When the Major's aircraft was down to a height of 457 metres and still 3 miles from the capital it was caught in searchlights and bombarded by flak. As fires raged on board and strips of metal began to fall off the starboard wing, Major van Eyssen and four of his men baled out successfully. They were captured by the Russians, flown to Moscow for interrogation, and eventually repatriated.

The rudder control and hydraulic system of Captain Bill Senn's Liberator were shot away, the upper gun turret holed and the nose set on fire. The Captain, his navigator and top gunner were all wounded, but he somehow managed to guide the plane back to Italy, landing without flaps or wheels. [3] The officer was awarded the Distinguished Flying Cross.

In two days, there were 54 sorties and 23 successes. Eleven aircraft were lost and the same number made unserviceable through damage caused by flak. Professor Mackenzie noted: 'At this rate there would soon be no long range aircraft or trained crews available for night operations from Italy.' [4] On 15 August, Air Marshal Slessor ordered a change in tactics. The airlift from Italy continued intermittently until 11 September, but on 2 October the Polish Resistance was forced to surrender to the Germans.

In a lecture to the South African Military History Society in 1983, Major van Eyssen pointed out that 'the Airlift failed in its purpose, but it served to cement a bond between Poles and South Africans based on mutual respect and sincere friendship.' [5]

Similarly, the present day South African Department of Defence records:

> 'The cost of the abortive SAAF "Warsaw Concerto" was tragically high in men and machines, but the daring and skill of the pilots and crew involved nevertheless earned SAAF the lasting respect and admiration of the Polish Resistance fighters. In 1992, 67 ex members of 31 and 34 squadrons were awarded the Polish Warsaw Cross for their role in the relief operations.'

Over 30 per cent of Allied air strength in Italy consisted of SAAF squadrons or South Africans seconded to RAF squadrons. In September 1944, SAAF air and ground crew totalled 17,271 officers and men.

On 12 October 1944, the SAAF bombers were deployed in 'supply dropping in northern Italy,' as the sortie reports record, aiding partisans who were defending liberated zones.

The planes were assigned in groups of five to four coded target areas. Three were in Piedmont: Parrot, south west of Turin, the regional capital, Dodge, south east of the city, and Chrysler, in the western surrounds of Lake Maggiore. The fourth DZ was Morris, north east of Genoa in the Ligurian Apennines.

Sixteen of the aircraft were from 31 Squadron and 4 from the 34th, each with an 8-man crew. After heavy losses during months of bombing, mine laying and supply drops, the squads were only kept up to strength by the inclusion of many RAF and some RAAF personnel.

The mission had already been postponed on several occasions due to bad weather, and the airfield was still waterlogged in places. Yet spirits were high when the Liberators lumbered into the sky between 4.05 and 4.40 in the afternoon. There had been no losses over Italian targets.

Captain Senn piloted one of the aircraft bound for DZ Chrysler, which was in what history would come to know as the Free Republic of Ossola. His navigator on KH 205 Y was fellow South African Lieutenant John Roos, who many years later told a reporter from the *Johannesburg Sunday Times* of the dramatic events that night:

> 'On the first leg of the flight across Italy, one of the aircraft developed a technical problem and turned back. The remainder had no difficulties. "Gee," the position-plotting radar with which they were all equipped, functioned perfectly and they crossed the Italian coast below Rome on course and on time.
>
> 'On the second leg, up the Italian seaboard towards Genoa, their problems started. Gee was useless there. A warm front, arriving much earlier than predicted, drew a veil of high cirrus clouds over the stars, making astro-navigation impossible. It also blanketed the sea in mist and low cloud, preventing conventional navigation. There was no way of determining drift, no way of calculating wind, no way of fixing position. Turning back was out of the question.
>
> 'They flew steadily on, using dead-reckoning navigation based on the meteorological forecast. But, as they searched the sky for enemy opposition, they did not realise that the warm front had completely upset wind predictions. And navigational error had set them on a collision course with the Alps. In the circumstances, the experience and wisdom gained on many flying expeditions was useless. With Corsica on their port beam, luck scratched a small hole in the clouds immediately below one of the aircraft – 205 Y. The hole was only just big enough for a wide awake crew to drop a flare and for their tail gunner to align his guns on the flickering light bobbing on the sea surface. Five degrees of starboard drift – five degrees against an expected fifteen.
>
> 'Alarm bells started ringing in the navigator's mind. The problem was whether he could accept the unconventional drift as being accurate. There was no way of checking it. To modify anticipated winds on the strength of a gunsight drift taken by someone else under poor conditions was really stretching things. A few deep, controlled breaths of oxygen settled flutters of panic. He could think clearly again. A quick calculation showed that if he used the drift and it was wrong they would come down 18 kilometres south of the target over level

ground. But, if it was right and he ignored it, they would overshoot the target by 48 kilometres. Much too close to the Alps for safety. Changing course was accomplished within minutes.

'Liberator 205 Y broke cloud dead on target, immediately above the huge black cross marked in the snow by the waiting partisans. The supplies went down, swaying at the ends of small parachutes. Mission accomplished, 205 Y headed back for base with all stops out.' [6]

The aircraft returned to Celone at 10.50pm after a round trip of six and a half hours. Twenty-five minutes later, the only other plane to make a successful drop on Chrysler arrived: EW 158 G, captained by Australian Flying Officer Max Badham with an RAF crew. There was just one more success on another target. By midnight, 14 Liberators had reached base, but 11 had been unable to drop their cargoes. Crews reported a scene of chaos as aircraft milled about in the darkness in the vain hope of glimpsing signal fires through the clouds.

An anxious wait began for the remaining six planes. In the morning there was only bright and empty sky. A seemingly endless list of airmen who had not returned appeared on the Mess notice board. No radio contact could be established with the aircraft and none had landed at emergency airfields.

Gradually news filtered through from Allied missions that two of the Liberators had crashed in Piedmont with the loss of all those on board. Partisans waiting on the ground reported that the planes had overflown the drop zones in dense cloud. Then there had been the chilling sound of distant explosions.

Liberator KH 239 S from 34 Squadron, flown by Flight Sergeant CW Lawton, RAAF, had crashed on level ground at Cantalupa. The aircraft had been assigned to the nearby DZ of Parrot. The other plane was KH 154 W of 31 Squadron, piloted by another Australian, Flight Sergeant DV Watson. The aircraft had been bound for DZ Dodge, but fell to earth at Rorà.

After the war, three more crash sites were found in Piedmont. The planes had been captained by South Africans from 31 Squadron. Liberator KG 874 J, flown by Lieutenant AHR Metelerkamp and assigned to Dodge, hit the hillside above Ostana. The two other bombers had been bound for Chrysler: KG 875 D, piloted by Captain L Von Beukes, located at Valprato Soana, and KG 999 P, flown by Lieutenant CP Nel, found at Ala di Stura.

Forty-eight airmen belonging to the SAAF, RAF, and RAAF, were lost on this one night, 40 from 31 Squadron and 8 from the 34th.

Various theories have been advanced to explain the tragedy. The aircraft faced some flak as they crossed the coastline near Genoa, but generally it was fairly light and lasted for less than a minute. Enemy night fighters had been withdrawn in September. So the cause probably lies in the perils of flying in submission to what the ill-starred French aviator and writer Antoine de Saint-Exupéry called 'those elemental divinities – night, day, mountain, sea and storm.'

One mystery still remains. The twentieth Liberator was never seen again after leaving Celone at 4.15pm. The aircraft had an experienced crew, six of whom had flown together on the mission to Warsaw by KG 858 H described earlier. Anne Storm, daughter of the bomb aimer on the missing plane relates:

> 'My father, Flying Officer Thomas Roberts (Bob) Millar, a member of the RAAF who served in 104 Squadron RAF and later 31 Squadron SAAF, was posted missing in action on 12 October 1944. His aircraft, Liberator KH 158 H, was one of the five assigned to DZ Morris. The pilot was South African Major SS Urry. The other crew members were: Lieutenants Armstrong and Collard, Second Lieutenant Lordan and Warrant Officer Bloch, all SAAF, and Flying Officer Hudspith and Sergeant Fitzgerald from the RAF.
>
> 'As a child living in Sydney I had always known that my father did not return from the war and that my mother, Beth, was a war widow. It was just something I accepted. There were many others in my position at Christmas parties organised by Legacy (similar to the British Legion) and at school.
>
> 'Then in January 2001 my mother told me of a notice she had seen in a Sydney newspaper asking for relatives of another of the pilots from 31 SAAF to contact the writer. There was to be a service in Bra, Italy, to remember the sacrifice these 48 young men had made.
>
> 'The mission had been researched by Giuseppe Barbero, an Italian who grew up with stories of the crashed planes, the search in the mountains and the furtive wartime burials of the crews while Italy was under German occupation. Former local partisans recalled that two of the SAAF Liberators had crashed at Rorà and Ostana. Together with Nick and Catherine Madina, an English couple with a holiday home

nearby, Beppe sought to document the partisans, the crews and the South African squadrons. Gradually the scope of the enquiry was widened to try to trace and contact all the relatives of the brave airmen who did not return from the mission. In April 2001 the City of Bra welcomed 21 family members to three days of moving commemoration and remembrance.

'I was delighted to attend together with my daughter, Elizabeth. At a civic reception at the start of the festival, I read out this letter which my father sent to me on 1 February 1944:

"My dear Daughter,

'This is the first time I have written to you and although you are as yet too young to read it, perhaps mother will store it up until the time comes when you can read it for yourself. In two days time it will be your first birthday anniversary – a great event for your parents. My regret is that I personally cannot be there to help you blow out your single candle, but believe me lassie I will be there in spirit.

'I am writing this from a place called Italy which is far away from our fair land – a place I would not be by choice so far separated from a wife and daughter so dear to me. But I am here, precious one, because there is a war on caused by certain people who wished to rule the world harshly and despotically, imperilling an intangible thing called democracy which your mother and I thought all decent people should fight for. You will understand as you grow up what democracy means to us and how it is an ideal way of life which we aspire to put into practice. 'All I ask of you, Anne dear, is that you in your life stay as sweet as your mother and cling tight to the subtle thing that we call Christianity, which has been the core of her way of life and her mother's and mine. I hope that you will love and respect me as I love and respect my father. 'That's all young lady. Have a happy birthday – may they all be happy birthdays. I hope to be home again one fine day. In the meantime lots of love to you and to mother.

"From Dad, Bob Millar."

'The ex-partisans were very moved by the letter and shook my hand. Many of them had also lost relatives and friends during the conflict. At that moment I truly felt part of the commemoration.'

The mystery of the plane's disappearance has yet to be solved.

NOTES

1. SAAF, *War Diary*, Container 44, File 1, p 5424.
2. Major JL van Eyssen, DFC, 'The Warsaw Airlift,' *S. A. Military History Journal*, December 1983.
3. Steve Stevens, DFC, 'Warsaw Airlift,' *FlyPast*, November 1997.
4. WJM Mackenzie, *The Secret History of SOE*, p. 524.
5. Major van Eyssen, DFC, op. cit.
6. John Roos, 'In Search of Charlie,' *Johannesburg Sunday Times Magazine*, 18 May 1985. The article is a moving account of the quest by Gunner Woody Nel for information on the loss of his older brother, Lieutenant (Pilot) CP Nel, who had flown another of the planes bound for Chrysler: KG 999 P, found at Ala di Stura.

7
The Ossola Rising

In September 1944 the Resistance liberated the first sizeable part of occupied Italy, the Ossola Valley, which links the western shore of Lake Maggiore and Switzerland. The free zone covered 1,600 square kilometres, 71 per cent of the present province of Verbana-Cusio-Ossola, with a population of 85,000, living in 35 communes. Its capital was Domodossola, the small frontier town at the entrance to the Simplon Tunnel on the main route from Milan to Berne and the junction for a narrow-gauge line to Ascona and Locarno.

The partisan offensive was conceived by the CLNAI in Milan in July, encouraged by the Allied summer onslaught and the capture of Rome. The plan was partly based on the knowledge that there were strong partisan formations to the west of Ossola around Lake Orta: the Garibaldini of Vincenzo Moscatelli (Cino) in the Sesia Valley and the Mountain Assault Brigade Filippo Beltrami in the Strona Valley. The brigade was named in honour of its first commander, who had been killed at Megolo on 13 February 1944, and was now led by Captain Bruno Rutto. At the beginning of August, the Germans were forced to agree to a neutral zone around Omegna owing to persistent attacks by these forces.

Across the river in Ossola was the Valtoce Division, led by tank officer Alfredo Di Dio, whose younger brother, Antonio, had also been slain at Megolo. Farther east was the Valdossola, commanded by Major Dionigi Superti, a former airman and director of a logging firm. His men were deployed among the rugged mountains of the Val Grande and had already received airdrops of weapons and supplies from the Allies.

To the north of Domodossola was a new communist division that had been created by Moscatelli and his friend Eraldo Gastone (Ciro). The Garibaldini commanders took part in a junta formed to direct military operations, but remained semi-detached members of the Resistance family.

In early August, a new formation also emerged in the Cannobina Valley, near the Swiss border. The Piave Division was led by officers Armando Calzavara (Arca) and Filippo Frassati (Pippo), who were already known to the Allies through their help to escaped prisoners of war.

The campaign to liberate Ossola began in the last week of August. Isolated garrisons in the mountains were overrun and the Cannobina Valley freed. The railway lines south and east of Domodossola were cut and the partisans operated part of the system using state employees and rolling stock.

By 1 September, most of the land north of Domodossola was under Resistance control. The partisans now forced the surrender of the garrisons crowded along the western shore of Lake Maggiore. On Friday, 8 September, coordinated attacks were launched on the few strong points and frontier posts still in enemy hands. By Saturday, Domodossola was isolated and surrounded by 3,000 partisans, some armed with 20-mm field guns. The garrison consisted of 500 German and Italian troops, mostly SS. A combative priest called Don Luigi Zoppetti urged the partisans to make the town the capital of a liberated zone from which the national uprising would radiate.

To avoid the streets flowing with blood the Church assumed the role of mediator. The senior priest, Don Luigi Pellanda, convened a meeting between the two sides. The German and Italian commanders offered to remove their forces provided they would not be disarmed. They also said they would not leave without the fascist administrators and their families. On behalf of the partisans, Dionigi Superti and Alfredo Di Dio agreed to allow the departure of the Germans with unloaded side arms, but made the fascists give up all their weapons, which were stashed in a barracks ready for Resistance use.

At dawn on Sunday, 10 September, a long column of German and Italian vehicles prepared to leave Domodossola. The partisans checked for heavy weapons and then gave permission for the convoy to leave for Fondotoce under escort. The Prefect of Novara, Enrico Vezzalini, told an angry Mussolini that 'not one shot was fired' in the defence of the town.

As the enemy left, the partisans entered, welcomed by the ecstatic population. A proclamation was read out to inaugurate the Free Zone of Ossola. A mild mannered surgeon, Professor Ettore Tibaldi, returned by special train from exile in Switzerland to become President. The unfolding drama was relayed to the world press by dozens of foreign journalists who flocked across the border. Eventually the Swiss Government granted the new zone diplomatic recognition and a veteran anti-fascist, Cipriano Facchinetti, became Ossola's ambassador in Berne. After the war, the experiment would become known as 'The Republic of Ossola.'

Major Dionigi Superti, leader of the Valdossola partisans, was entrusted with the task of creating a Provisional Governing Council, *la Giunta Provvisoria di Governo*. Half of its members were drawn from the partisan brigades and the remainder from the residents of Domodossola and the surrounding countryside. All the councillors were nominees of the various political groups, ranging from communists and socialists to monarchists and Catholics. Housed in the Palazzo di Città, the assembly began an ambitious programme of reform based on democratic ideals. Meanwhile, councils were re-established in the other communes, together with trade unions. On 18 September, the Governing Council introduced a daily newspaper and soon the political parties and even some of the partisan formations began to publish their own bulletins.

Fascist laws and institutions were abolished and new ministries created overnight. A socialist lawyer, Ezio Vigorelli, became Minister of Justice. He introduced a legal system that safeguarded the rights of detainees, including the fascist prisoners held at Druogno in the Vigezzo Valley. In the field of education, enrolment for 200 local schools began on 25 September, with a new term set to commence on 16 October. A commission was set up to design a new curriculum.

While the politicians made ever more changes including new street names, the people were more concerned with problems of survival. There was a shortage of money and basic necessities and rations were low. Italian writer Giovanna Giannini noted that ten days after the occupation of Domodossola only 500 litres of milk a day were available for the population of 14,000. Not even one sack of flour arrived from the plain owing to the German blockade and trains from Switzerland came loaded with political exiles but not with foodstuffs. Fortunately, the Confederation did eventually agree to supply 200 quintals of potatoes a day on a commercial basis and a great deal of help was provided by the Swiss and Italian Red Cross.

The lack of finance was gradually alleviated by funds supplied by SOE and OSS, the minting of metal tokens by local industries, and the printing of paper coupons by the *Banca Popolare di Novara*, which were redeemed by the new Italian Republic after the war. The stock of RSI postage stamps was overprinted 'CLN – Ossola Libera – 10.9.1944.'

Defence of the zone was the most critical problem. A local militia was created, led by Colonel Attilio Moneta, a native of Malesco. General Bianchi, the Italian military attaché in Berne, sent down a number of volunteer regular officers who had crossed the border on the 1943 Armistice and had been interned. On 18 September a Council of War was established, though it never functioned effectively owing to political differences and clashes of personality. A deputation arrived from the CVL, headed by General Cadorna. He insisted on the need for a coordinated plan of defence and a unified command, even offering to take on leadership himself. This was rejected by the communists. However, the decision was made to transform the Council of War into a Supreme Command. A three-times decorated officer of the Italian Lancers from Cuneo, with the alias of Colonel Delle Torri, proper name Giuseppe Curreno di Santa Maddalena, was appointed Chief of Staff.

On 12 September, the Beltrami and Garibaldini formations had forced the fascist garrison of Omegna to flee to Gravellona Toce, which was itself taken two days later. However, the enemy still held the surrounding mountains. The partisans constructed three lines of defensive positions in this sector.

The greatest military need was for weapons and ammunition as captured supplies would soon run out in the face of any enemy counter-offensive. Two weeks before the start of the revolt, Colonel Attilio Moneta had contacted John McCaffery, SOE head in Switzerland, and had won guarantees of British assistance. Now the time had come for words to be turned into deeds.

At the outset, the Allied secret services in Switzerland had been ordered to do all they could to prevent the creation of the free zone. A letter sent by John McCaffery to Ferruccio Parri of the National Liberation Committee on 27 September reveals the British attitude to the rising:

> 'You must not pretend to be in charge of military operations like Alexander and Eisenhower … Some time ago I said the greatest contribution you could make was continuous, widespread sabotage. I have only supported you at Domodossola because I recognise the moral

value of it for Italy. The partisans have fought well but they want to be one of the Allied armies. Who has asked you to do so? Not us.' [1]

McCaffery wrote later that the partisans had been 'bitten by the bug' of proclaiming an independent area. He and the OSS head in Switzerland, Allen Dulles, had eventually agreed to support the plan, but only so as 'not to undermine the morale of the partisans.' The Foreign Office in London voiced its disapproval. [2]

As a result, Allied help was somewhat low-key. Lieutenant George Paterson, a Canadian attached to the British Army, was sent as liaison officer. He had taken part in the first commando raid in Italy, Operation Colossus, in February 1941. Eleventh SAS Battalion destroyed the Tragino Aqueduct, but the entire party was captured shortly afterwards. Following the 1943 Armistice Paterson escaped from a train, was recaptured, broke out of the San Vittore prison in Milan and finally crossed into Switzerland.

The officer was recruited by SOE in Berne two or three days after the revolt began, as related by John Windsor in his book *The Mouth of the Wolf*. Paterson's brief from John McCaffery was mainly to arrange parachute drops to the partisans:

> 'At the moment they are all right for weapons, but if it starts to roll and recruits swarm in we'll have to get arms, ammunition and supplies to them by airdrop. That's one of the reasons why I need a man like you right on the spot.'
>
> 'There's another?' queried Paterson.
>
> 'Yes, this one is political ... these few square miles are the first in Italy to be free and under their own control for more than twenty years ... How are they going to handle themselves? Will they cooperate to govern or will they break up into factions with the possibility of civil war? This may give us some clue as to what will happen in the country as a whole once Jerry is finished.'

At the Lieutenant's request, he took Corporal Jack Watson with him as radio operator, second in command of his section during Operation Colossus. They had met again at the Swiss quarantine centre at Bad Lostorf. The pair were sent to Locarno and about a week later McCaffery's subordinate, Major John Birbeck, drove them to the border.

Three partisans were waiting on the other side. Their leader, John Windsor wrote, was 'a middle aged man, lean, grey-haired with a bristling moustache and the look of a soldier.' He greeted Paterson: 'Let me welcome you to Free Italy. I'm Colonel Moneta, formerly of the Royal Sardinian Cavalry, and I am to be your liaison officer with our partisan brigades.'

The agents were taken the few miles to the Italian's home village of Malesco to meet the partisan leaders, Dionigi Superti, Alfredo Di Dio and Armando Calzavara. There was one notable absentee. Vincenzo Moscatelli had sent word that he was too busy to attend.

Over the next two weeks the partisans advanced southwards, averaging three or four miles on a good day. The soldiers in the isolated German garrisons in their path showed little appetite for a fight. Their equipment was taken and they were bundled over the border. Paterson was surprised at the lack of enemy response and every day expected to hear that a fighting battalion had moved into the area. When this did not happen, he surmised that all the front line troops were trying to stem the Allied offensive from the south.

During lulls in the fighting, the Lieutenant visited the partisan formations. He finally met Moscatelli and was impressed by his drive and determination, but also noted that 'his force, like the others, lacked trained officers and NCOs, and was equally disorganised and unpredictable.'

Once Domodossola was captured, Paterson witnessed chaotic meetings of the Governing Council:

> 'No one had any money to feed more than three thousand very hungry partisans. Cattle and supplies were commandeered, much to the annoyance of the peasant farmers and civilian members of the council, while the Professor, caught in the middle, had increasing difficulty in keeping the various factions from each other's throats.'

At one such heated meeting the Canadian decided to take a trip back to Locarno. He told the assembly: 'It will be quicker that way to arrange airdrops of weapons and ammunition, and I can tell them that we desperately need money to pay for supplies.'

Professor Tibaldi replied: 'Impress on them that a government without money is like a well without water.'

The agent crossed the border, contacted Major Birbeck and returned next day with twenty million lire and a precious schedule of airdrops. When Paterson officially handed over the currency to Professor Tibaldi in Domodossola, he found himself the hero of the hour. Even Vincenzo Moscatelli congratulated him at this token of good faith on the part of Russia's allies.

The partisan leaders were also delighted at the opportunity to boost their firepower. The first parachute drop was planned for three days later. Lieutenant Paterson joined Armando Calzavara and a dozen of his men from the Piave on a flat-topped hill north of Domodossola to await the consignment. The night sky was clear and serene, but as the appointed hour came and went no throb of aircraft engines broke the spell.

The agent apologised to Calzavara, but he only laughed and said: 'If things ever went right in this war, then we would really be concerned. Let's go back to town and have breakfast. We will try again three nights from now.'

Blending our different pieces of information, we know from the previous chapter that the reason for the non-appearance of the aircraft was that the SAAF Liberators assigned to Ossola had been grounded by bad weather over Celone. When flights were able to resume on 12 October, two aircraft made successful sorties, one aborted its mission, and two crashed in mountains to the west with the loss of all those on board.

There would be no further opportunities for supply drops to the liberated zone.

The inevitable counter-offensive against Ossola was led by German SS General Tensfeld. His task force included 500 of his countrymen, but was mainly composed of detachments from the National Republican Army and auxiliaries of the locally recruited Black Brigade, the *6th Augusto Cristina* of Novara.

Estimates of the size of this unit vary widely, from 3,000 to 13,000, but what is certain is that about 5,000 partisans were outmanned and outgunned in every sector where they opposed the enemy and were forced to fall back on new positions in the mountains.

After some diversionary thrusts from the south, the main attack began in the east. Early on 12 October, Colonel Moneta roused Lieutenant Paterson with the news:

> 'Word has just come down from Malesco that a whole German battalion, Alpine troops, and some fascist infantry have got across Lake Maggiore and landed near Cannobio. We had a patrol in the area and they could do nothing but fall back into the mountains. They blew the bridge through the pass and that may slow the Germans down a little. Di Dio is up there, assembling his brigade at Malesco, and he's going

to move forward at dawn to try and halt them in the pass. If we don't stop them there, they'll be in behind us along the frontier and then …'
He drew a finger across his throat.

A car was found and Paterson drove the Colonel and Corporal Watson the 30 miles to Malesco. They arrived at first light, but the partisans had already marched out in the direction of Finero. The Corporal was instructed to stay in the village. If things went wrong, he was to return to Switzerland and tell Major Birbeck.

The Lieutenant drove on until he reached a long straggling column of five or six hundred men. They were the zone's mobile reserve, formed from one of the two brigades of the Valtoce and reinforcements from the Piave. The guerrillas told the Canadian that Commandant Di Dio and his officers had driven ahead to reconnoitre the bridge destroyed by their forces the previous evening.

When Paterson caught up with the leaders, they asked if he would like to go along. He agreed as he feared that any hesitation on his part might be misinterpreted. However, the agent thought it was folly for the officers to push on so far ahead, particularly as the mission was best undertaken by a scouting patrol. '*In bocca al lupo*' (good luck), he replied. In English: 'In the mouth of the wolf,' giving John Windsor's book its title.

The group had to walk the last five hundred yards to the bridge. As they discussed plans to surprise the advancing Germans it suddenly became apparent that it was they who had fallen into a trap:

> 'All hell broke loose. From somewhere high on the ridge heavy machine guns stuttered into life … Then they saw the distant column disintegrate into a multitude of running figures as the fire tore into the ranks and the men dived for safety.'

The two cars were hit and their petrol tanks exploded. A culvert under the road provided the only shelter. George Paterson and some of the Italians managed to dash to safety, but Alfredo Di Dio was cut down in the attempt. When the Germans finally rushed the position after two hours, Colonel Moneta was also slain. The Lieutenant had run out of ammunition and threw his tommy gun down. Angry Germans began to kick and punch him, a rifle butt caught him across the head and he passed out.

When the Canadian came round, he faced two soldiers who had cocked their rifles for his summary execution. A Sergeant Major yelled at them to stop. Prisoners were to be taken for interrogation. Lieutenant Paterson was eventually returned to the San Vittore in Milan. In a letter to Major Birbeck that was smuggled out of the prison, the agent wrote: 'It was partly my own fault getting caught. Let my natural instinct be overridden by a burst of Italian enthusiasm.'

General Tensfeld's men also advanced swiftly in the west. On 13 October an armoured train from Baveno and the Italian infantry scattered the main partisan force in the lower Toce valley. At 5.40 in the afternoon the following day, enemy troops re-entered Domodossola. The streets were almost deserted as more than half the population had fled. Three special trains had taken hundreds of civilians and partisans across the border to Ascona. The refugees were sent to Basle and on to camps in central Switzerland. The final clashes took place along the frontier on 23 October. After only 43 days the liberated zone was no more.

A few hundred partisans led by Colonel Delle Torri and Vincenzo Moscatelli evaded the enemy and gradually resumed military operations. On 24 April 1945, the Resistance finally liberated the Ossola zone and moved into western Lombardy.

Four days later, Milan, 'Capital of the Resistance,' was freed. At one in the afternoon, the communist brigades entered the city, led by a shiny, black open touring car and seven captured tanks. Among the crowd was the SOE agent George Paterson, newly released from prison. The Canadian suddenly realised that the man waving from the rear of the car was Vincenzo Moscatelli. The communist leader saw him at almost the same instant, and shouting to his driver to stop, jumped out and rushed over:

> 'Giorgio,' he beamed, shaking hands enthusiastically, 'I thought the worms had you months ago. This is a surprise, and on such a great day for Italy. Come along, you've got to ride with me. You should be in the parade. I want to hear your story.' [3]

NOTES

1. John McCaffery, "No Pipes or Drums", unpublished diary, quoted in Richard Lamb, *War in Italy*, p. 217.
2. Richard Lamb, *War in Italy*, pp. 215–16.

3. John Windsor, *The Mouth of the Wolf*, pp. 130–224. For his work with the Resistance, George Paterson was promoted captain and awarded the Military Cross with two bars. In addition, he was granted the Freedom of the City of Milan. The narrator of his story in the 1967 book, John Windsor, had been blinded when serving with the Canadian Armoured Regiment in Italy.

8
Cherokees in Piedmont

Special Force Cherokee Mission parachuted into northern Piedmont on the night of 17–18 November 1944. The target, codenamed Adstone, was in Zimone, a small village near the mill town of Biella – known as 'the Manchester of Italy.'

Heading the operation was Major Alastair Macdonald, who had previously served with the French Resistance. The other officers were explosives and sabotage expert Captain Jim Bell and Lieutenant Patrick Amoore, a skilled linguist who had been in Italy since the invasion and was afterwards promoted to captain. Corporal (later sergeant) Tony Birch was the wireless operator.

In a signal to base Lieutenant Amoore reported:

> 'Our drop was successful, though I landed in the middle of a pigsty between two large pigs that climbed over the wall in their excitement. I had dropped fourth and last which accounted for my narrowly missing the roof of a farmhouse situated outside Adstone DZ, this being achieved by pulling on the right hand lift web which pushed me a yard to the right in time. DZ Adstone is not ideal for body dropping, being rather too small. All the other members of the mission landed well. The DZ was attacked two hours afterwards by the fascist garrison of Cerrione, but the thrust was beaten off.' [1]

The very arrival of the mission was a tonic to the partisans. For more than a year they had been forced to rely on weapons captured from the enemy. Airdrops had been meagre owing to Allied suspicion of left-wingers:

'They formed the 5th and 12th Garibaldi divisions and the Justice and Liberty brigade,' Alastair Macdonald related. 'The total force exceeded three thousand men. But the Garibaldini formations were separated from us by the city of Biella, which was surrounded by blockhouses. The communists were spread around the Mosso Valley, north east of Biella, while we had landed to the south west of the city on a morainic wooded ridge known as la Serra. It soon became apparent that a move from one area to another involved either a long and tortuous night march or a risky journey by car along a piece of very open road.' [2]

The communist leaders told their superiors: 'The mission seems quite well pleased with us. The organisation which the British found here, the discipline and the order, were better than anything they expected. Or at least this is what they say. It seems that the Allied commanders have assigned the Biella area an important role to the extent of placing it at the centre of a large-scale operative plan which has as its main objective control of the Aosta Valley on the Liberation.' [3]

The success of the project depended on boosting the firepower of the Resistance. So, in Alastair Macdonald's words, the 'first task was to find a larger and more easily defensible drop zone and to organise a big parachute drop of arms and explosives destined for the main partisan formations.' [4]

The choice for the new drop zone fell on a snow-covered plateau surrounded by high mountains, but it proved too difficult for aircraft to reach. As an alternative the partisans proposed a flat area at Baltigati in the commune of Soprana, north east of Biella. The site was high enough for the accesses to be safeguarded, but was also clothed in thick woods. This seemed to have compromised the plan until a clever solution was devised. Partisans approached sympathisers on the council and they readily agreed to announce a charitable initiative. The commune asked for 'volunteers' to cut the trees down in order to provide firewood for the needy during the harsh winter. Dozens of eager helpers appeared as if from nowhere and in two days completely deforested the site without raising the enemy's suspicions.

A test drop was made to the field on Saturday, 16 December. The mission was a complete success. On the same day sorties were also flown to the Justice and Liberty brigade in the plain, but the enemy managed to seize part of the consignment. The lesson was clear. The communist partisans prepared a detailed plan to defend a belt several kilometres wide around the site at Baltigati. Arrangements were made to cut telephone and telegraph lines and to carry out diversionary actions on lower ground. Squads of helpers were assembled, transport mobilised and collection points prepared.

Confirmation of the airlift came through on Tuesday, 26 December – Saint Stephen's Day in Italy. The organisation was scrambled, though many partisans were rather sceptical after past disappointments. But an hour before sunset a squadron of Liberator bombers arrived over the Sessera Valley. The fascist garrison at Lessona fired random shots into the sky as multicoloured parachutes began to rain down on the hills.

The supply drop was the largest by Special Force during the campaign. Alastair Macdonald listed the contents as 165 Bren guns, 505 Sten guns, 565 rifles, 5,725 Pigna hand grenades, 85 infantry mortars and 80 Piat anti-tank grenade launchers, in addition to ammunition, explosives, fuses and detonators. The haul was eventually divided among the communist divisions, the Justice and Liberty brigade, and the Cherokee Mission itself. To make the most of the equipment, reinforcements arrived at DZ Adstone: Sergeant Major Johns of the Royal Engineers, who trained the partisans in the use of explosives, and Sergeant Bell, namesake of the second in command, Jim Bell, whom he assisted in sabotage and demolition.

Captain Bell had already targeted a railway bridge outside the German Headquarters in Ivrea, the largest town of the neighbouring Canavese district. The line was of great strategic importance as it was used by trains carrying special steel munitions from the mines and foundries at Cogne in the Aosta Valley. The bridge was only 90 metres long and guarded at both ends, so the venture appeared almost foolhardy. Nevertheless, an Italian technician with the alias of Alimiro volunteered to lead a squad to place the charges.

Alastair Macdonald recalled: 'When I shook his hand before he left and wished him good luck, he just said: "Remember one thing, Major, if I fail this time I don't think I'll get a second chance." [5] However, he succeeded, and an entire span of the bridge thundered into the Dora Baltea river. The structure was still not fully repaired when the war ended.

In early January 1945, Major Macdonald returned to la Serra amid signs of an imminent enemy offensive. Shortly afterwards, a busload of German non-commissioned officers was ambushed and killed near Cerrione by a communist brigade whose men were eager to use their new weapons.

The day after the attack, the commander was in the nearby village of Magnano:

> 'I was chatting with the radio operator from SIM known as Armando and a despatch rider whom I had not seen for some time, while our courageous ex-prisoner of war, Corporal Keith Jones, kept watch from a hilltop.
>
> 'One moment everything was peaceful, the next a detachment of *Waffen SS* had burst upon the village in a surprise attack. The courier was able to save herself by running like a hare, but Armando and I could not move quickly enough in the deep snow that surrounded the village and almost immediately we came under rifle fire. Armando was fatally wounded in the shoulder by a fragment. He had been about to be withdrawn from duty after long and arduous service.' [6]

The Major was captured. After a period of detention in the civilian gaol at Biella, he was sent for interrogation to the headquarters of the German Security Service, the SD, in Verona. The partisan leader Ferruccio Parri occupied a nearby cell. Alastair Macdonald managed to convince his gaolers that he was simply an escaped prisoner of war and was sent to the transit camp at Mantua. He escaped before he could be sent to Germany and fled towards Lake Garda with the help of a boy of ten or eleven years old:

> 'He saw me emerging from a garden and recognised the British army trousers I was wearing under my civilian overcoat and told me to turn round and follow him to the shore of the River Mincio, which formed a vast lake by the camp. There he got me to climb into a boat and rowed me across under the eyes of the German guards.' [7]

Alastair Macdonald eventually reached the Camonica Valley and crossed the border to Switzerland.

Before being taken prisoner, Major Macdonald had asked Patrick Amoore to make contact with the famous communist partisan Vincenzo Moscatelli whom he had already briefly visited at his base on Lake Orta. Amoore was also to liase with an American OSS mission operating in the area, which was codenamed Chrysler.

The officer finally met Moscatelli in the Sesia Valley and the Italian escorted him to a villa on the lake where the Americans were sheltering. Also there were agents from another OSS operation, codenamed Mongoose, who had a disturbing story to tell. Their commanding officer, Major William Holohan, had mysteriously disappeared and was believed to have been killed in action. However, It came to light after the war that the Major had been brutally murdered, allegedly by his colleagues, though the case was never properly resolved in court.

When Patrick Amoore returned to la Serra at the end of January, he learned that Major Macdonald had been captured, and found himself in the middle of a savage round up. His first twenty-four hours were spent in the village of Sala Biellese, hiding behind a hen house that led to an open-air toilet. Police sniffer dogs called to the scene were so disgusted by the smell that their handlers pulled them away after a token search of the area. Blackshirts set fire to the surrounding dwellings, including a villa that concealed Radio Liberty, the partisans' local service. The operatives managed to escape by the skin of their teeth, fleeing through the kitchen door with their transmitter in the direction of the woods.

Shortly afterwards, the two remaining British officers met to discuss tactics. Patrick Amoore discovered that in his absence Jim Bell and his men had put the railway line between Biella and Santhià out of action with the partial demolition of another bridge at Salussola. It was decided that the team would now leave the area to coordinate sabotage and anti-scorch measures in the Canavese district and the lower Aosta Valley, while Patrick Amoore would accompany the partisan command to ensure Allied directives were implemented. Instead, as he related, in the weeks that followed it was more a question of survival:

> 'We were constantly hunted across the deep snow and in biting cold. For food we often only had a few dried chestnuts. To avoid anyone learning of our whereabouts we had to keep on moving from one area to another by night, especially as the authorities were offering large rewards to informers and posters were on display everywhere.' [8]

The fugitives finally found sanctuary at Azeglio in the lower Canavese district. Patrick Amoore and corporals Birch and Jones were given hospitality in the castle of Count d'Harcourt, ex-fascist mayor of Turin. Then, when the nobleman's trembling steward was on the verge of a nervous breakdown, they moved to the basement of the village church. Contact had been lost with the partisan command, but one day in early March the Chief of Staff made a surprise appearance. He expressed his delight that the agents were unscathed, but above all wanted to know when new airdrops of weapons would be made. Patrick Amoore told him they would only be possible when a more secure site was found and the weather had improved.

A new drop zone was soon prepared on the margins of la Serra at Torrazzo. The site was given the codename of Perth in honour of the birthplace of the POW Corporal Keith Jones. On 18 March the DZ received Major Robert Readhead, the mission's new commanding officer. He was accompanied by an Italian captain, Marco Folchi-Vici, who used the alias of Mark Terry. The original force of 4 agents had now grown to 16, as well as a varying number of escaped prisoners of war.

Patrick Amoore remained close to la Serra to supervise the reception of a flood of men and materials that began to descend on Perth in preparation for the final battle.

The Allied attack on the Gothic Line resumed on the Fifth Army front on 5 April 1945 with a push towards La Spezia. In the middle of the month the Free French also began an offensive across the Maritime Alps. On 20 April, the new German commander in Italy, General von Vietinghoff, ordered the Italo-German Liguria Army of Marshal Graziani to retreat – action which within days would bring it into conflict with the partisans of Aosta, Ivrea and Biella.

According to the withdrawal plan, codenamed Autumn Mist, the army's two corps – the Lombardia and the 75th – would rendezvous south east of Milan before making for the Veneto. The detachments had orders not to surrender to the partisans or the liberation committees, but only to the Allies.

On 24 April, the partisan military commanders in Piedmont issued their order for a general uprising in directive E 27. It included instructions to impede the German retreat and to prevent the destruction of power stations and other facilities. On the same day the partisans stormed into Biella. The German garrison surrendered at Vercelli on 26 April and the fascist headquarters in Aosta gave in two days later.

The Lombardia Army Corps led by *General der Artillerie* Kurt Jahn withdrew from the Ligurian Riviera and Maritime Alps and crossed the River Po near Valenza as planned. [9] In contrast, the two divisions of the 75th Army Corps of General Ernst Schlemmer, which had been based in the western Alps, first had to regroup near Turin on Saturday, 28 April.

General Jahn had negotiated a truce with the Alessandria partisans that allowed his troops to cross the river without facing battle, but General Schlemmer failed to clinch a similar deal at Turin and his corps was forced into a time consuming detour around the city. Meanwhile, the garrison fled and concluded a pact with the partisans at Tronzano Vercellese.

On Saturday afternoon partisans from Santhià observed soldiers from the 75th Corps retreating east along the Turin-Milan motorway towards Novara. The column took three hours to pass. It was led by tanks and half-tracks, but after repeated attacks by Allied aircraft and clashes with partisans there was a shortage of vehicles and fuel and many men were on bicycles or walking. Ahead of the force, the partisans disrupted roads and destroyed bridges along the Cavour Canal.

Late in the evening the retreat suddenly ground to a halt and the troops began to occupy local villages. The partisans had orders not to attack the invaders in view of the great disparity in numbers, but the Germans massacred almost 60 civilians and members of the Resistance in Cavaglià and Santhià and raised many dwellings to the ground.

The soldiers created a defensive barrier along 30 kilometres of the Elvo torrent between Salussola and Santhià to allow the regrouping of the corps south of Ivrea. At the centre of the line was a motorway bridge at Carisio where anti-tank weapons had been concentrated to prevent Americans from Milan crossing the stream. The civic leaders were held as hostages in the town hall to ensure the compliance of the locals.

During Monday afternoon a German major arrived at the bridge and reported that the Liguria Army had surrendered to the American 4th Armored Corps. General Pemsel, the Army's Chief of Staff, had signed the document a few hours earlier at Castiglione Di Stiviere, near Lake Garda. The Major was rushed for an audience with General Schlemmer at his headquarters in the castle of Mazzè. However, the commander angrily dismissed the capitulation, saying it was 'contrary to military honour.' Meanwhile, American aircraft bombarded his troops with copies of the surrender document translated into several different languages. [10]

At the centre of the German-held pocket in Ivrea, religious and CLN leaders tried to persuade General Schlemmer to capitulate. He stubbornly refused, saying that he did not trust the partisans. But when on Tuesday a column of 70 tanks from the American First Tank Division reached the bridge at Carisio, the General finally changed his mind. He sent his Chief of Staff, Colonel Faulmüller, on a desperate journey to contact the Cherokee Mission. The commanding officer, Major Readhead, had moved with Captain Terry and the radio operator Corporal Birch to Vercelli, the provincial capital. So it was an unsuspecting Captain Amoore who was left holding the fort, as he related after the war:

> 'On 2 May 1945 I was the guest of Count Carlo Trossi, the noted Italian racing driver at his castle in Gaglianico, a few miles from Biella. The reason I was there was to have my first hot bath in over five months – a very necessary experience. Suddenly there was a knocking on the door and Trossi shouted: "You're wanted at the Albergo Principe (the temporary headquarters of the Cherokee Mission)." We had taken over the former German HQ which also had a convenient restaurant. I was needed because a German surrender delegation had arrived by car under partisan escort from their HQ in the Canavese and were offering the unconditional surrender of the 75th German Army Corps commanded by General Ernst Schlemmer.
>
> 'I arrived at the Albergo Principe and there was a large crowd outside. I went upstairs to Cherokee HQ and there interviewed the Chief of Staff, Colonel Faulmüller, together with his assistant. He handed me a document signed by General Schlemmer offering the unconditional surrender of all of his troops. I first consulted with the partisan area commanders present. They were undecided whether to accept as their bitter experiences during the past couple of years did not induce trust in the Germans. However, in the circumstances a quick decision had to be taken so that hostilities should cease. It was decided the unconditional surrender would be accepted by the partisan command and by myself as representative of the mission on behalf of the Allies. The Germans, including fascist troops and ancillaries, were estimated at over 100,000 men.
>
> 'Through our two interpreters, I stated our terms of surrender. Just after the first paragraph had been typed, two senior American officers appeared. Colonel John M Breit, together with his Staff Major, of the US Armored Group (whose spearhead had just reached Biella) had

come forward on a personal recce in a command car. He enquired who was in command and upon introducing myself he asked for a situation report. I explained that we were in the process of drafting the unconditional surrender of the 75th German Army Corps. After discussing it with his ADC, he turned to me and said: "That's OK by us, go ahead." [11]

The hard-won triumph of the Cherokee Mission was crowned when its first chief, Major Alastair Macdonald, returned to Biella as Allied Military Governor.

NOTES

1. TNA: PRO HS 6/840.
2. Patrick S Amoore and Alastair Macdonald, 'La missione Cherokee nel Biellese, Due testimonianze,' *l'impegno*, April 1992. The translations of this and other Italian sources are mine.
3. Claudio Dellavalle, *Operai, industriali e partito comunista nel Biellese, 1940/1945*, pp. 248–50.
4. Amoore and Macdonald, op. cit.
5. Ibid.
6. Ibid.
7. Ibid.
8. Ibid.
9. General Jahn was captured by the Allies on 1 May 1945. He was transferred to Camp 198 (Special Camp 11) at Island Farm, Bridgend, South Wales, and held as a POW until 1947.
10. Ezio Manfredi, 'Dalle Alpi occidentali a Santhià, La strage dell'aprile 1945 e la resa del 75° Corpo d'armata,' *l'impegno*, December 2001.
11. Laurence Lewis, *Echoes of Resistance*, pp. 132–5. Colonel John M Breit, commandant of the American 135th Infantry Regiment, is also mentioned in my book, *Escape from Italy, 1943–45*.

9
From the Mountains to the Sea

On Thursday, 18 January 1945, British Clover Mission, made a perfect daylight landing on the south eastern slopes of the highest peak in northern Liguria, Monte Antola (1,597 metres), north east of Genoa. The DZ was controlled by the Americans and a six-man OSS team commanded by a 'Major Van' dropped at the same time. They took on responsibility for supplies and training, while the British handled intelligence, tactical planning, liaison with the CLN and the regional military command, and political matters generally.

The Special Force mission was the main one for Liguria, part of Lombardy south of the River Po, known as the Oltrepò Pavese, and the Piacenza province of Emilia. There were also four sub-missions, led by Captain Bentley in Imperia, by Major Johnston in Savona, after the capture of five other agents, by Captain Irwin in Voghera, and by Major Stephen Hastings in Piacenza. Another mission was already established in the Ligurian province of La Spezia under the former POW Major Gordon Lett, which was controlled by TAC HQ in Florence. The story of the last two missions is told in my book *Escape from Italy, 1943–45*.

The British Liaison Officer was Lieutenant Colonel Peter McMullen, whose family has run the firm of McMullen and Sons, Hertfordshire brewers, since 1827. In his official report, he wrote:

> 'I was lucky enough to have as my second-in-command Major (now Lieutenant Colonel) Basil Davidson, with whom I had worked previously. He not only spoke fluent Italian and German, but also had considerable knowledge of Italian affairs.' [1]

The Major was already an accomplished journalist, having worked on *The Economist* and the *Evening Star*, among other publications, before being recruited to special operations in December 1939. His many books include *Special Operations Europe*, published in 1980, which includes both a colourful account of the mission and a commentary on the differing beliefs and intentions of the partisans and the Allies.

Sir Stephen Hastings, MC, wrote in his 1994 autobiography, *The Drums of Memory*, that Lieutenant Colonel McMullen 'had a real knowledge of the oddities and limitations of guerrilla war and no illusions at all ... Peter came of a conventional, conservative, county family and his political views were entirely consistent. Basil was an intellectual and a Marxist – albeit a romantic one. This would not have mattered except for the fact that all partisan life is governed by politics and the mountains were full of well-organised communist bands. It was much to the credit of Peter and Basil that their political disagreements were never bitter and their mission an unqualified success.' [2]

Completing the team were an Italian officer, Lieutenant Wochiecevich, and Corporal (later sergeant) George Armstrong, radio operator on Davidson's last mission in Yugoslavia.

Basil Davidson provides a nice description of their arrival:

> 'The journey was short and comfortable. No long distance dropping at night any more, but a leisurely start after breakfast from an airstrip near Leghorn. No hours of crouching in a stone-cold fuselage, but twenty minutes' pleasant flying up the coast beside the shining blue Tyrrhenian, 1,500 metres below, before turning inland with an umbrella of four British Spitfires larking overhead. And then across peaks and folds of frozen mountains, climbing from the Riviera, until the pilot found his signals on the ground and slowed and fell to 170 metres or so. And at last a leap and sunlit drop to a land of lovely snow.
>
> 'A group of partisans was waiting in the snow.' [3]

Two of the men introduced themselves as Miro and Marzo. Davidson recalled that neither had any marks of rank, nor even uniforms apart from a red scarf, but that both were armed. They were in their forties. Miro, the younger, was Antonio Ukmar from Trieste. A railwayman by occupation, he had visited the Soviet Union and fought as a guerrilla in Spain, Ethiopia and France. In the summer of 1944 Miro had arrived to lead the partisans of the Sixth Zone. Marzo was Giovanni Battista Canepa, a journalist from nearby Chiavari. He had been imprisoned by the fascists many times and had also fought with the Garibaldi Brigade in Spain. Following the 1943

Armistice Marzo had formed one of the first armed groups, the famous band of Cichero, taking its name from a little hamlet in the mountains.

The British mission was taken along snowbound slopes to a huddle of cottages perched on the upper slopes of Monte Antola at Capanne di Carrega. The partisans had made their headquarters in the inn, which was half cottage, half refuge. The SOE men stayed three days. In his official report on the mission, Peter McMullen recalled: 'The partisans' welcome was very cordial, and we had the impression that they were more than a little surprised to receive such an apparently imposing mission after what had seemed to them to be long months of neglect on our part.'

The special operations team had a dual role: liaison between the partisan formations and 15th Army Group, and, when the enemy withdrew, between the new civil administration and the Allied Military Government.

The directives from the Army Group for phase one were:

(1) The primary target should be intelligence of enemy order of battle, movements, intentions, minefields, etc.
(2) Partisan formations should be encouraged to carry out sharp stinging attacks on enemy columns, command posts, etc, without risking their hand in large scale operations, which, it was argued, would only result in their rapid elimination as a fighting force.
(3) Partisans should in every case prepare themselves for an all-out effort in conjunction with an eventual Allied offensive, the signal for which would be given by the Army Group Commander.

Support from the partisans appeared a remote prospect in January 1945. The Lieutenant Colonel wrote:

> 'During late November and the whole of December, the enemy had driven with considerable forces throughout the whole great quadrilateral formed by the seacoast, Route 62, Routes 9 and 10, and Route 35. Many partisan formations had suffered so badly as to have gone virtually out of business altogether, some for the time being, but others, it appeared, for the duration.
>
> 'The enemy had used a large part of the 162nd Turkestan Division and considerable Republican and fascist forces. Learning by experience, they deployed them in multiple columns converging on prearranged points over a period of weeks, and often also doubling back on their tracks.

'Whatever liaison there had been between the provinces of Piacenza and Genoa had ceased to exist, and the difficulty was further increased by the arrival through the lines of the only American team (Walla-Walla) active in that area. We therefore landed with a large question mark before us.'

The mission learned that the partisan force numbered between 2,000 to 2,500 men. There were four main formations. The largest was the Cichero Division, with six brigades east of the Scrivia Valley and along the Levante Coast. Two of these units had suffered badly in the enemy offensive. The other brigades were more or less intact, but tired and somewhat dispirited. The Americano Division was deployed along the Bobbio to Voghera road. Its five brigades were all badly knocked about. It is doubtful if the division numbered 500 men and most of its equipment had been lost to the enemy. The Mingo Division with three brigades in the west was also greatly weakened and scarcely in a position to fight anyone. Finally, there was a unit of about 200 men, called the Mobile Brigade Caio, which was centred on Santo Stefano d'Aveto. It had moved with its commander, Istriano, from the Val Nure in Piacenza.

Lieutenant Colonel McMullen related that:

'Nine tenths of the formations of the Sixth Zone were Garibaldini and the remainder mainly *Giustizia e Libertà* – Action Party. The zone command and the commands of the Garibaldi brigades were predominantly communist, however it must be clearly said that this does not mean that the leaders were all communists or that the rank and file were mostly communist.

'The leading personalities on the zone command were undoubtedly communists of conviction and of long experience, by no means crude hotheads, who understood their absolute need for collaboration with the Allies and with non-communist elements among Italians themselves. Their strength lay precisely in their own wealth of political experience, their high standard of discipline and political understanding, and the support of their party, which was very highly organised in Genoa ...

'On the whole we found remarkably little political trouble.'

Basil Davidson recalled: 'We had dropped in the wake of one major enemy sweep across these mountains, and, as we soon found out, on the eve of another ... Troops under German officers now aimed not so much at destroying partisan units, which they found difficult, as at robbing the partisans of village support by terrorising the villagers, which they found easy.' [4]

In his summary, Peter McMullen wrote:

> 'The enemy's flagging interest was apparently whipped up to new efforts by the exaggerated stories he received of waves of Allied parachutists landing in the mountains. He came after us and following one or two undignified withdrawals we kept moving at almost daily intervals for two or three weeks. But given the excessively broken nature of the ground we were usually at least one jump ahead of the nearest column and this enabled us to keep open our contact with base and to send a large volume of traffic …
>
> 'The general position in the area occupied by Cichero, into which we had dropped and in which for various reasons we decided to make our headquarters, was bad. Enemy drives had been very successful in disrupting the internal organisation, confidence and morale of all these formations. The season was winter and a cold winter with deep snow at that. There was little or no prospect of the long expected Allied offensive, and perhaps most important of all, the partisans had no Allied liaison mission …
>
> 'We found therefore that the zone command had decided to cut its losses for the rest of the winter season, to cease its previous and by no means unsuccessful attempt to hold an occupied area in the mountains around Monte Antola free of the enemy, and to revert to the sketchiest form of partisan warfare until better times should come. It is fair to add that they themselves were not in the least demoralised and had no intention of making pacts with the enemy, though there was no lack of opportunity as far as the enemy was concerned. The partisans had already anticipated Army Group directive to cut formations to minimum size by sending home all those who had weakened during the recent drive and who grumbled at winter conditions. The comparatively few who remained were all the better for that.
>
> 'The arrival of Allied missions with the promise they held of recognition and of supplies put fresh heart into them … Our presence meant that it would be worthwhile, perhaps even necessary, to hold the enemy out of a certain chosen area in a more or less permanent way. The partisans fixed on the complex of mountain ridges linked with the passes at Capanne di Caregga and Capanne di Pei. Heavy snowstorms sealed this

decision by making movement almost impossible.

> 'The tide was turned by a famous action in the upper Val Borbera on 30 January when a German column of 32 men was captured intact, with one officer and all their equipment. The *rastrellamento* continued with varying fortunes until the middle of February, but morale was already rising and this success was followed rapidly by others of the same magnitude. By the end of February, the number of German prisoners held was a problem in itself.
>
> 'Another factor making for improved morale was the slowly awakened sympathy of the peasants. The men in the formations were almost all from the towns, mainly Genoa. They had little knowledge of, or interest in, peasant ways and the peasants responded by resenting their intrusion and the additional dangers it meant for them. This lack of sympathy was occasionally acute. On the whole it seems to have decreased as the spring approached and in the end there was even cordiality.'

Basil Davidson recalled: 'By the middle of February couriers from Miro found us with the news that his units had passed to the counter-offensive. Reaching him again, we learned that there had been plenty of hard fighting around Antola, up the valleys leading from the plains and from Genoa. We had seen nothing of that, but at least we had learned the terrain. We were beginning to feel at home in these mountains.' [5]

The offensive phase began in the Sixth Partisan Zone in the second part of February. Lieutenant Colonel McMullen wrote:

> 'We decided that in view of the time factor it would be best to concentrate on the areas of greater tactical importance to the east of the Scrivia Valley and on the problem of Genoa itself. We had been able to forward several couriers via Major Lett (and later Major Henderson) through the lines and our W/T link remained extremely good.
>
> 'The formations to the east of the Scrivia were by this time receiving ample, and perhaps more than ample, supplies of all kinds of equipment dropped by parachute. Their morale had vastly improved. The worst of the winter had past and the enemy had showed decided signs

of having had enough of it. It was agreed with the Zone Command, therefore, to push their units closer down to their main targets – the lines of communication and prisoner-taking points. We decided to reinforce our missions. Major Johnston, Captain Brown and Flight Lieutenant Rippingale accordingly arrived with necessary W/T operators and equipment on 21 March. [The Major headed the sub-mission to Savona and the other officers formed another satellite mission in Piacenza]. Base was informed that SAS or commando teams could be used to advantage.

'The enemy's position was weakening. It was true that he had now got the whole of 135 Fortress Brigade, reinforced by large numbers of navy personnel who had gone through short infantry and anti-tank training courses, deployed around Genoa, mainly on anti-partisan duties. In addition, there were two battalions of *Bersaglieri*, one to the east and one to the west of Genoa, and part of 162 Division available for *rastrellamenti*, as well as local Black Brigades and Republican troops drawn from the provincial depots at Genoa, Alessandria and Piacenza.

'But all this was clearly unequal to a large-scale drive. All the enemy could do was to perpetuate his attempts to contain our formations by a series of more or less unrelated strikes. The partisans continued to take due toll of his columns and in the three months ending mid April it is fair to put the casualties they caused him in the area east of the Scrivia at something in the region of three thousand. We were able to interrogate more than two hundred German prisoners during this time and had a fairly complete picture of the enemy's order of battle …

'The changing balance produced a position in which by 5 April when Army Commander ordered all-out effort for formations east of Route 45, we had occupied and freed practically the whole central mountain area east of the Scrivia, and were ranging as far as Route 62, where formations of other zones were active.

'The orders of 5 April met with a genuine effort to embarrass the enemy who remained along the littoral and in successful actions various formations cleared the enemy out of his remaining advanced points. The Coduri Brigade was active on Route 1 itself and actually occupied Sestri Levante for some hours. Formations in the Cichero area had by that time moved right down into the Scrivia Valley and were harassing the enemy on both sides of the main roads. In the Oltrepò Pavese, the formations commanded now by Edoardo, with Captain

Irwin as liaison, were also busy on the Via Emilia (Route 10) and down to the Po itself. Morale was high.

'My own mission had meanwhile been strengthened by the arrival by parachute on 14 April of Captain Gordon, Lieutenant Richards, RNVR, and two W/T operators. A few days later we were also joined by Captain Murphy, RAMC, who had walked up from the Spezia area, via the Piacentino, having collected some very useful medical intelligence on the way. Captain Gordon with one W/T operator was sent off at once to join Coduri Brigade and report on the position in the area of Chiavari, and he was able to send us valuable information on the progress of the battle ... An Italian officer, Lieutenant Quattrocolo, was also dropped to us at this time for courier duties: we formed a very good impression of his abilities and sense of duty.'

On the eve of the final offensive, the original core mission of 4 had grown to 16, made up of 5 British officers, 4 'other ranks,' 3 ex-POWs and 4 Italian officers.

As the prospect of liberation came ever closer, the part the Resistance would play became the main topic of discussion. On 10 April, the Communist Party issued its famous Directive 16, which led directly to the signing of the order for the national uprising by all five parties in the CLNAI. The main points of the directive read:

(1) Partisan formations will attack and eliminate Nazi-Fascist headquarters and effect the liberation of cities, towns and villages ... the appropriate organisations will proclaim a general strike ...
(2) The enemy will be faced with the following alternatives: 'Surrender or die.'
(3) On no account whatsoever must our comrades in military or civil bodies accept any proposal or advice or consider any plan designed to limit, prevent or obstruct the national uprising. A combination of firmness, tact and skill must be employed in all discussions with Allied military missions which have chosen to be the mouthpiece for those who favour a wait and see attitude, and are therefore inclined to attach too little importance to our urgent requests for the arms and

ammunition needed to ensure the success of the insurrection. In the circumstances, we must be prepared to face the fact that the Allies may decide for one reason or another to withhold their support, instead of making the contribution for which we have asked.'

The Ligurian Liberation Committee had finalised its own 'Plan A' for insurrection about a week earlier. It provided for a full-scale assault on enemy positions in all the towns of the Riviera, especially Genoa. The plan brought the Resistance directly into conflict with the intentions of the Allies.

The partisan military command in the region had already provided its commanders with guidance on relations with Allied missions. On 25 March, the CVL stated that their General Command in Milan had stressed that it was essential for them to ensure the personal safety of the members of the missions and to collaborate as closely as possible with them. However, the guidance also mentioned the necessity to uphold the spirit of national dignity and some formations, said the leaders, had behaved in a way that was incompatible with this principle:

> 'Certain partisan commands have failed to realise that the function of the Allied missions, which act as liaison organisations between us and the Allied Command, is purely the giving and receiving of information. The missions have no direct military authority and therefore the proper procedure is not to beg them cap in hand for the material needed at air bases but to request them to supply us with what is needed to strengthen a movement that is operating in the immediate interest of the Allies.'

Basil Davidson related: 'Our own orders at this stage were brief and clear about tasks to be carried out. So far as Genoa and its installations were concerned, these were to secure maximum effort by the CLN and its fighting units in an enterprise called anti-scorch. This meant the planning and eventual carrying out of actions to prevent enemy demolition of ports, railways, tunnels, public installations and the rest.' [6]

On 9 April, Lieutenant Colonel McMullen delivered his orders to the members of the CLN, which amounted to the exact opposite of their 'Plan A.' Basil Davidson recalled: 'We were told to instruct the Cichero Divisions not to go down into the towns, and above all not to go down against the enemy in Genoa.'

Remo Scappini, a communist artisan who was President of the six-party Ligurian CLN, wrote in his memoirs, entitled *Da Empoli a Genova* (From Empoli to Genoa), that the mission made a 'drastic intervention' in the plans for insurrection, stating that it wished 'to clarify the attitude of the Allied High Command to the entry of partisan forces into Genoa and other cities. The principle to be observed in every case is the following: a minimal number of partisans must enter the city and remain there.' Scappini added: 'The principle was decisively rejected by the committee and its regional commanders.'

As Basil Davidson related, the mission eventually worked out a compromise plan:

> 'In a long radio message to the 5th Army, Peter recommended agreement on a rising within the city, aimed at anti-scorch, that would be backed by the rapid infiltration of 300 picked fighting men from the mountain units ... I cannot recall that we ever received any comments, favourable or otherwise. The rising in Genoa began and then continued upon the quite different and altogether larger "Plan A" of Miro's command. It stands on the record that British warships did in fact make a naval demonstration off Genoa on the third day of the insurrection. Though too late to be of any use, this was the Allies' sole contribution to the whole remarkable affair.' [7]

Lieutenant Colonel McMullen wrote that as early as 15 April the German commander, General Meinhold, 'had made tentative approaches through the Cardinal of Genoa, suggesting that some agreement be reached whereby in return for his refusal to destroy public services, he would be allowed to withdraw his troops without molestation by the partisans.'

On 20 April, General von Vietinghoff, the German commander in Italy, issued his order to retreat across the River Po, Operation Autumn Mist. General Meinhold was instructed to proceed as swiftly as possible along the valley and to make for the Veneto. On the morning of 23 April, Peter McMullen wrote, 'the General made a more definite approach to the Cardinal, saying that he needed three or four days in which to withdraw and undertaking not to allow extensive demolitions. The Cardinal referred this to the CLN Liguria who replied that they would not treat with the enemy.'

As night fell, the Liberation Committee ordered a general insurrection throughout the city of Genoa.

NOTES

1. TNA: PRO HS 6/843 BLO's Report: Liguria. Lieutenant Colonel RP McMullen, DSO, MBE, May 1945.
2. Sir Stephen Hastings, MC, *The Drums of Memory*, pp. 114–15.
3. Basil Davidson, *Special Operations Europe*, pp. 279–80.
4. Ibid., p. 287.
5. Ibid., p. 292.
6. Ibid., p. 333.
7. Ibid., p. 339.

10
The Grand Finale

At first light on Tuesday, 24 April, the partisan rising began in Genoa and across Liguria. Towns north of the city and along the coast road fell to the partisans, the railway lines were cut and public installations secured.

Savage fighting raged in the centre of Genoa around Piazza De Ferrari and in the port. Seven thousand German troops and a similar number of fascist soldiers and auxiliaries faced some 3,000 partisans. Two thirds of the irregulars belonged to communist formations, with the remainder in groups controlled by the Christian Democrat and Action parties.

Lieutenant Colonel McMullen related:

> 'The urban partisans (SAP) came out in force, secured arms from the enemy to reinforce the few they had already, and succeeded in cutting the main enemy groups off from each other.'

Telephone wires and water and electrical supplies to the garrisons were severed and transport disabled. German columns were also blockaded in tunnels on the road to Milan and their situation was deteriorating.

From his headquarters at Savignone, north of the city, General Meinhold issued a threat to order his artillery on Monte Moro and in the port to bombard the city unless his troops were allowed to retreat. The CLN decided to counter the ultimatum with one of its own: 'The moment a shell explodes in the city, we will execute the troops we have captured.' The enemy guns stayed silent. However, as Tuesday closed the position of the partisans seemed perilous. The mountain formations were at least a day's march away and the Americans had only just reached La Spezia, over 100 kilometres farther down the coast. General mobilisation was ordered in Genoa and secret recruiting posts were set up in four different sectors.

By daybreak, 3,000 civilians had been enrolled in a makeshift partisan army.

Peter McMullen recalled:

> 'Meanwhile, word had been got out to the mountain units and the four small brigades which according to previous arrangement would infiltrate into the city in a state of emergency began their march. From the north east, brigades Balilla and Severino came in through the Bisagno and Polcevera valleys. And from the north west the Pio and Buranello brigades came down into Sestri Ponente and Sampierdarena.
>
> 'On 25 April, the Sixth Zone command received definite confirmation of the rumours of insurrection and according to the agreed plan, certain units began to move on Genoa while others opened up in full strength on the Scrivia Valley communications and down towards Route 1.'

Shortly before midday an ambulance from Genoa drove up to the German Headquarters at Savignone. Hidden in the back of the vehicle was a leading member of the Resistance, Carmine Romanzi of the Action Party. The partisan handed two letters to General Meinhold, one from the CLN demanding his surrender, the other from Cardinal Archbishop Boetto of Genoa soliciting a peaceful solution.

The General reluctantly agreed to meet the Liberation Committee and was driven to Genoa in the ambulance, led by two partisan outriders. During the journey the commander handed Romanzi his pistol. Accompanying the General were his Chief of Staff, Captain Asmus, and a junior officer, Joseph Pohl, who acted as interpreter. They were taken to Cardinal Boetto's seat, the Villa Migone at San Fruttuoso. Waiting at the residence were the German Consul, Von Hertzdorf, and the partisan representatives: the communist Remo Scappini, Liberals Doctor Giovanni Savoretti and the lawyer Errico Martino, and Major Mauro Aloni, military commander.

Negotiations began at 5pm. About the same time, a large number of the enemy surrendered in the port. During the discussions it was revealed that the partisans now held 1,360 German prisoners.

General Meinhold finally agreed to surrender. Remo Scappini related that after hours of indecision the German signed almost impetuously at 7.30pm. The witnesses had the impression that the commander had carried out the most important duty of his life.

The surrender document reads:

It has been agreed that:
(1) All the German Armed Forces on land and sea under the command of General Meinhold surrender to the Armed Forces of the CVL belonging to the Military Command of Liguria.
(2) The surrender will be carried out by the troops giving themselves up to the nearest partisan units and handing over their weapons.
(3) The Liguria CLN undertakes to treat the prisoners according to International Law, with special regard to their personal property and conditions of internment.
(4) The Liguria CLN will consign the prisoners to the Allied Anglo-American command operating in Italy.

Four copies were made: two in Italian, two in German.
Meanwhile, as Lieutenant Colonel McMullen related:

> 'Major Davidson with Attilio, the Commissar of the Zone Command, set off from Torriglia to see how far they could get towards Genoa. They rode right down into the centre of the city, past block after block posted by the suburban SAP, without hindrance except for sporadic sniping. Contact was made immediately with the Regional Command and with the CLN. Major Davidson found all the public services working and the newspapers on the point of going to press.'

Local sources time Major Davidson's arrival at the College of San Nicola, temporary home of the CLN and the military command, at half past midnight. The officer heard of the enemy capitulation from Errico Martino, who said: 'The Germans have surrendered. To the CLN, to us.' The news was immediately signalled to Fifth Army Headquarters in Florence, though inexplicably it was never passed on to the advancing Americans in the 92nd Infantry Division.

The unit, nicknamed the Buffalo Soldiers, had been activated as the only black American infantry division in Europe, albeit with white senior officers. However, after months of fighting around the Gothic Line only one black regiment, the 370th, remained in the division. It was brought up to strength by the 473rd Regiment, made up of white anti-aircraft gunners turned infantrymen, and by the motorised 442nd Regimental Combat team, formed from Nisei soldiers – descendants of Japanese immigrants. The 92nd was now affectionately known as the 'Rainbow Division.'

At 9 in the morning on Thursday, 26 April, a prominent Christian Democrat, Paolo Emilio Taviani, reached the radio station at Granarolo and announced the surrender over *Radio Genova*. After reading the text of the capitulation, Taviani added: 'People of Genoa, rejoice! The insurrection, your insurrection has succeeded. For the first time in the course of the war a well-trained and well-armed army corps has surrendered to the people. Genoa is free. Long live the Genoese! Long live Italy!'

However, considerable firing was still going on in the city. Large bodies of enemy troops were resisting or at least had not capitulated.

Lieutenant Colonel McMullen recalled:

> 'General Meinhold had surrendered a few hours beforehand, but had made it clear that he could not answer for all his troops since he had now been out of touch with them for many hours. In fact several garrisons refused to acknowledge his orders. Colonel Klein, commanding some 2,000 men in the port, actually held a court martial in which General Meinhold was condemned to death as a traitor.
>
> 'In the morning, the CLN held a solemn ceremony of investiture of the Prefect in the newly liberated Prefecture and Lieutenant Colonel Davidson (whose promotion had been advised the night before) was invited to witness this. It was the first occasion upon which the whole CLN – consisting of 18 members when non-party representatives are included – had met together in one place and recognised each other.
>
> 'Just as this rather moving ceremony was closing, news came in that all three major garrisons still resisting were in course of trying to force a junction. It seemed the situation might be critical in view of the relatively tiny number of partisan troops in the city.
>
> 'As it turned out, about 1,000 enemy succeeded in making their way westwards from the German Naval HQ at Nervi as far as the skyscraper at Foce di Bisagno, east of the port, where they blockaded themselves in and waited upon events. Another 2,000 in the port made a bid to break out and were held. A third party, some 300 strong, surrounded in Sampiedarena, blew up a large ammunition dump, killing a substantial number of civilians, as a means of diversion, while they tried to break out from an adjacent point. They too were held by reinforcements hurried down from Pontedecimo and Bolzaneto in any transport that could be found. By the afternoon, the position had greatly eased.

'At about 16.00 hours, Lieutenant Colonel Davidson went with Miro of the Zone Command and Colonel Farini of the Regional Command to induce the surrender of the 1,000 naval ranks at Foce di Bisagno. They undertook to surrender at 10.00 hours the following morning and this undertaking they carried out.

'Meanwhile, the port garrison of 2,000, probably aware of the approach of Allied columns – by then already a short way west of Rapallo – thought better of their resistance and surrendered unconditionally to partisan formations after throwing a large number of their arms into the water. No port installations were blown up, but several small block-ships had already been sunk. By the evening, there remained in the immediate vicinity of the city only the batteries on Monte Moro which eventually surrendered to Commander 92nd Division, the group at Sampierdarena which also surrendered on the 27th, and a group at Pontedecimo which also held out until the following day.

'At 21.00 hours on the 26th, Lieutenant Colonel Davidson got on the telephone to the command post of 473 Regiment of 92 Division at Rapallo and reported the situation. At 23.00 hours I arrived myself and decided to go towards Rapallo at once to meet advanced elements. I took with me one member of the Regional Command and did in fact effect a junction near Ruta.

'During the course of the morning of the 27th, American troops began to flow into the city and the battle was over. The Divisional Commander was the first to admit that the partisans had taken the city before his troops had time to get there. He expressed surprise at the complete public order and arranged an immediate meeting with the CLN to congratulate them on this. The anti-scorch programme had been realised almost in its entirety – a result that was beyond the wildest expectations of any of us. Genoa on that day, as previously, had light, water, public transport, newspapers, radio transmissions from the local station, and so forth, and the main roads prepared for destruction by the enemy were open for as much transport as cared to pass.

'In other sectors things had gone equally well. Coduri Brigade had mopped up enemy posts round Carasco and penetrated to Chiavari which Allied elements were then nearing. Caio and Berto brigades made forced marches on Genoa and arrived by the evening of the 26th. Iori Brigade was in by the same morning, having less ground to cover.

Division Pinan occupied the whole Scrivia Valley from Busalla to Tortona and took Novi and Tortona on the 26th and 27th. Units of the Oltrepò Pavese took Voghera, cleared their zone completely and crossed the Po. Division Mingo occupied the Turchino Pass and helped in rounding up isolated garrisons.'

The first meeting between General Edward M Almond, the commanding officer of the American 92nd Infantry Division, and the Liberation Committee took place at the Hotel Bristol at one in the afternoon on 27 April.

Basil Davidson recalled that there was an initial misunderstanding:

'Tell them,' General Almond said, 'that my troops have liberated their city and they are free men.'

'A silence followed: which continued.

'The General looked at me with some surprise: couldn't I speak the language?

'Then Providence intervened, or the sacred law, or whatever you prefer to think may now and then take pity on the frailties of humankind and stop collisions in the avenues of time. There came, from outside that room, the sudden din of shouts and uproar.

'We rushed through the floor to ceiling windows to a balcony giving on that stretch of arcades.

'Looking down, we saw far up the street the dense fore-ranks of a crowd of advancing men, and then we saw it was a column, a column of German prisoners a dozen or more abreast, hundreds of them, thousands of them, marching down that street unarmed but with armed partisans on either side …

'At my elbow, General Almond said nothing, but he looked. The prisoners came on down that street, an endless column, for it turned out afterwards that more than 14,000 German and fascist prisoners had been taken in Genoa alone. And the people in the arcades continued to clap and cheer.

'Then we went back into the salon and General Almond gave me a measuring glance and said "All right." And then he made a speech that warmed the heart. He had known nothing of what to expect, but of this he said no word. Instead, he praised and thanked the CLN for what they and their troops had done.' [1]

Roberto Battaglia, the historian of the Italian Resistance, described the revolt in Genoa as a 'model insurrection.' There is a deceptive symmetry to events: the order for the rising was given on 23 April, the General surrendered on 25 April and the Americans entered the city on 27 April. However, as Basil Davidson underscored, the liberation of Genoa 'began as a desperate affair on the evening of 23 April, and it continued as a desperate affair. Only three days later did it climax in a final and huge success.' [2]

Lieutenant Colonel McMullen wrote:

'The taking of Greater Genoa from the enemy and the more or less simultaneous liberation of the whole neighbouring territory was an achievement which astonished no one perhaps more than those who carried it out.

'Many factors combined to make it possible. First among these was the almost complete disintegration of the enemy under the speed and success of the Allied advance, coming as it did on top of long and demoralising months of waiting in Italy while the German homeland was being invaded and overrun. Waiting, moreover, in a partisan infested country.

'General Meinhold, commanding the fortress of Genoa, surrendered himself and all his troops virtually without resistance. Had he not done so, but had he shared the die-hard views of some of his officers, there is no doubt he could have destroyed the public services of Genoa and caused severe losses to those who might have attacked him. Still it is fair to add that an important factor in his decision to surrender, as indeed he admitted in conversation with us, was his certainty that his troops would be subject to sustained and general attack by partisans during retreat.'

On Thursday, 3 May, the day after the guns had fallen silent across Italy, a victory parade of partisans and American troops was held in Genoa. Over the next three weeks, Basil Davidson helped his friend write his report on Clover Mission. Peter McMullen's account ends on a typical note:

'It would be ungracious to conclude this brief summary of events without some reference to the outstanding courtesy and kindness which I and the other members of my mission were shown after liberation by partisans of all ranks and formations.

'We were invited to numerous ceremonial occasions, directly or indirectly in our honour. At the end, on 16 May, together with Lieutenant Colonel Davidson, Sergeant Armstrong, 'Major Van' and the W/T operator of the OSS mission, and five partisan commanders, I was presented with the freedom of the City of Genoa. The name above mine in the city records reads "Mussolini," and that is being erased. Above that is Guglielmo Marconi.' [3]

The experience of war dissolved in such moving ceremonies across Italy, a symbolic ending and the affirmation of ties which still endure.

NOTES

1. Basil Davidson, *Special Operations Europe*, pp. 363–4.
2. Ibid., p. 344.
3. TNA: PRO HS 6/843 BLO's Report: Liguria, Lieutenant Colonel RP McMullen, DSO, MBE, May 1945.

Bibliography

Battaglia, R, *The Story of the Italian Resistance*, London: Odhams Press, 1957.

Churchill, WS, *The Second World War, Volume V, Closing the Ring*, London: Penguin Books, 1985.

Dellavalle, C, *Operai, industriali e partito comunista nel Biellese, 1940/1945*, Milan: Feltrinelli, 1978.

Davidson, B, *Special Operations Europe, Scenes from the Anti-Nazi War*, London: Grafton Books, 1987.

English, I, editor, *Home by Christmas?* privately published, 1997.

Foot, MRD, *SOE, Special Operations Executive, 1940–1946*, London: Pimlico, 1999.

Hastings, Sir S, *The Drums of Memory*, Barnsley: Leo Cooper, 2001.

Lamb, R, *War in Italy, 1943–1945, A Brutal Story*, London: Penguin Books, 1995.

Lett, G, Rossano, *An Adventure of the Italian Resistance*, London: Hodder and Stoughton, 1955. New edition published by Hugh Brian Gordon Lett, 2001.

Lewis, L, *Echoes of Resistance, British Involvement with the Italian Partisans*, Tunbridge Wells: Costello, 1985.

Macintosh, C, *From Cloak to Dagger, An SOE Agent in Italy, 1943–1945*, London: William Kimber, 1982.

Mackenzie, WJM, *The Secret History of SOE: The Special Operations Executive, 1940–1945*, London: St Ermin's Press, 2002.

Pickering, W, with Hart, A, *The Bandits of Cisterna*, London: Leo Cooper, 1991.

Prati, G, *La Resistenza in Val d'Arda*, Piacenza: Casa Editrice Vicolo del Pavone, 1994.

Procacci, G, *History of the Italian People*, Harmondsworth: Pelican Books, 1973.

Robertson, KG, ed., *War, Resistance and Intelligence, Collected Essays in Honour of MRD Foot*, Barnsley: Leo Cooper, 1999.

Scappini, R, *Da Empoli a Genova*, Milan: La Pietra, 1988.

Tudor, M, *British Prisoners of War in Italy: Paths to Freedom*, Newtown: Emilia Publishing, 2000.

Tudor, M, *Escape from Italy, 1943–45, Allied Escapers and Helpers in Fascist Italy*, Newtown: Emilia Publishing, 2003.

Various authors, *No. 1 Special Force and Italian Resistance*, Bologna: University of Bologna, 1990.

Wilkinson, P, & Astley, JB, *Gubbins and SOE*, London: Leo Cooper, 1993.

Windsor, J, *The Mouth of the Wolf*, London: Hodder and Stoughton, 1967.

Index of Names

Alexander, HR	17, 29, 54
'Alimiro,' technician	63
Almond, EM	86–7
Aloni, M	82
Amoore, P	61, 64–6, 68–9
'Armando,' radio operator	64
Armstrong, G	71, 88
Armstrong, Lieutenant	43, 48
Asmus, Captain	82
'Attilio,' commissar	83
Badham, M	47
Badoglio, P	4–5, 24–5
Baldi, D	13–15
Baldi, M	13–15
Baldi, P	13–14
Balduzzi, Doctor	17
Ballard, Captain	38
Barbero, G	48–9
Battaglia, R	26, 87
Bell, J	61, 63, 65
Bell, Sergeant	63
Beltrami, F	14, 51
Bentley, Captain	70
Bianchi, General	54
Birbeck, J	55–6, 58–9
Birch, A	61, 65, 68
Bloch, Warrant Officer	43, 48
Boetto, Cardinal Archbishop	79, 82
Bonomi, I	23, 25
Breit, JM	68, 69n
Brown, Captain	76
Bruen, EJD (Paddy)	11
Cadorna, R	26, 31, 54
Calzavara, A (Arca)	52, 56–7
Canepa, GB (Marzo)	71–2
Chamberlain, N	1
Churchill, O	26
Churchill, W	1, 4–5, 25
Collard, Lieutenant	43, 48
Croce, B	18
Croft, A	16
D'Alcorn, O	7–9
Dalton, H	1–2
Davidson, B	70–88
D'Harcourt, Count	65
Di Dio, Alfredo	14, 51–2, 56–8
Di Dio, Antonio	14, 51
Donovan, W	39
Doyle, C	2
Dulles, A	55
Durrant, JT	34
'Edoardo,' partisan leader	76
Eisenhower, DD	4, 54
Facchinetti, C	53
Farini, Colonel	85
Faulmüller, Colonel	68
Fischer, E	19
Fitzgerald, Sergeant	48
Folchi-Vici, M (Mark Terry)	66, 68
Foot, MRD	3, 36
Frassati, F (Pippo)	52
Gastone, E (Ciro)	51
Giannini, G	53
Giovanni, OSS operative	37
Goldingham, M	9–12
Gordon, Captain	77
Graziani, Marshal	66
Gubbins, C	1–2, 17
Gubbins, M	17–18, 22n

Harding, General	17	Millar, TR	43, 48–9
Hastings, Sir Stephen	41, 70–1	Millard, Corporal	37
Henderson, Major	75	Moneta, A	54, 56–8
Holdsworth, G	16–17, 21	Montezemolo, GL di	39
Holland, JFC	1	Moscatelli, V (Cino)	51, 56, 59, 64–5
Holmes, S	2	Munthe, A	18
Holohan, W	65	Munthe, M	17–18, 22n
Hope, A	22n, 37	Murphy, Captain	77
Hudspith, Flying Officer	48	Mussolini, B	4–5, 10, 23, 88
		Nel, CP	47, 50n
Irwin, Captain	70, 77	Nel, W	50n
'Istriano,' commandant	73	Niccoli, N	19
Jago, Regimental Sergeant Major	8	O'Connor, R	7
Jahn, K	67, 69n		
Jefferis, MR	1	Pajetta, G	31
Johns, Sergeant Major	63	Parri, F	24, 26, 30–1, 54, 64
Johnston, Major	70, 76	Paterson, G	55–60
Jones, K	64–6	Pellanda, Don Luigi	52
		Pemsel, General	67
Keany, J	22n, 37	Pickering, W	36–8
Kesselring, Field Marshal	19	Pizzoni, A	24, 31
Klein, Colonel	84	Pohl, J	82
		Procacci, G	29–30
Lauri, F	35		
Lawton, CW	47	Quattrocolo, Lieutenant	77
Lett, G	38, 70, 75		
Levi, P	9	Readhead, R	66, 68
Lockey, Sergeant	43	Ricciardi, A	7
Longo, L	26, 30	Richards, Lieutenant	77
Lordan, 2nd Lieutenant	43, 48	Rippingale, Flight Lieutenant	76
		Romanzi, C	82
MacCloskey, M	40	Rommel, Field Marshal	5
Macdonald, A	61–5, 69	Roos, J	46
Macintosh, C	16–22, 35	Roosevelt, President	4, 39
Mackenzie, WJM	27, 32, 36, 45	Roseberry, CL	3–4, 17
Macmillan, H	17	Rutto, B	51
Madina, C & N	48		
'Major Van'	70, 88	Saint-Exupéry, A de	48
Mallaby, R	4	Salvadori, M	18, 21, 24, 27, 37–8
Marconi, G	88	Santa Maddalena, GC di	54, 59
Martino, E	82–3	(Colonel Delle Torri)	
Mattison, JK	41n	Savoretti, G	82
Mauri, E	36	Scappini, R	79, 82
McCaffery, J	3, 17, 24, 54–5	Schlemmer, E	67–8
McDermott, ER	20	Senn, W	44, 46
McMullen, P	39, 70–88	Sogno, E, Count	17, 30–1, 37
Meares, J	11–12	Slessor, Air Marshal	45
Meinhold, General	79, 81–2, 84, 87	Storm, A	41, 43, 48–9
Metelerkamp, AHR	43, 47	Superti, D	51–3, 56

Index of Names

Taviani, PE	84
Tensfeld, General	57, 59
Tibaldi, E	52, 56
Togliatti, P	25
Tompkins, P	32
Trossi, C, Count	68
Turner, HS	41n
Turner, LL	41n
Ukmar, A (Miro)	71, 75, 85
Umberto, Crown Prince	25
Urry, SS	43, 48
Van Eyssen, J	44–5
Vassalli, F	39
Vezzalini, E	52
Vigorelli, E	53
Vittorio Emanuele III, King	24–5
Von Beukes, L	47
Von Hertzdorf, Consul	82
Von Vietinghoff, General	66
Walker, EV	13–15
Watson, Doctor	2
Watson, DV	47
Watson, J	55, 58
Willis, AGR	11, 15n
Wilson, M	31
Windsor, J	55, 58, 60n
Wochiecevich, Lieutenant	71
Zoppetti, Don Luigi	52